Hertford Museum
Celebrating our Centenary

edited by

Colin Harris

The Rockingham Press

First published 2003
by The Rockingham Press
11 Musley Lane,
Ware, Herts SG12 7EN

Copyright © 2003, Hertford Museum
Copyright © 2003 in all signed articles remains with the authors

All rights reserved. No part of this publication may be reproduced, stored in a retrieval system or transmitted, in any form or by any other means, electronic, mechanical, photocopying, recording or otherwise, without the prior permission of the publishers and copyright holders.

**A catalogue record of this book is available
from the British Library**

ISBN 1 873468 96 2

Printed in Great Britain by
Biddles Limited
Guildford & King's Lynn

CONTENTS

	Frontispiece: The alabaster crucifix from Layston	4
	Preface by Colin Harris	5
1.	*The Andrews Family* by Rosemary Bennett	6
2.	*A History of the Building and Garden* by James Nall-Cain	14
3.	*The Development of the Museum* by Ann Kirby	22
4.	*Bull Plain: a Brief History and Memories* by Jean Purkis	30
5.	*The Museum in the 1940s: a Childhood Recollection* by Edgar Lake	39
6.	*The Social History and Ethnographic Collections* by Helen Gurney	43
7.	*The Postcard and Photograph Collection* by Margaret Harris	47
8.	*'Paper' Collections* by Rosemary Bennett	56
9.	*The Hertfordshire Regiment and other Military Items* by Rosemary Bennett	63
10.	*Hertford Museum Archaeology* by Clive Partridge	66
11.	*Clocks and Scientific Instruments* by Edgar Lake	72
12.	*The Geology Collection* by Margaret Harris	76
13.	*The R.T. Andrews Trade Token Collection* by Edgar Lake	82
14.	*Friends of Hertford Museum* by Alan White	87
15.	*Looking Forward* by Helen Gurney	90
	Index	94

CONTRIBUTORS

Rosemary Bennett	Recently retired Curator of Collections at the Museum
Helen Gurney	Curator of Hertford Museum appointed in February 2002
Colin Harris	Chairman of Museum Trustees since 1996
Margaret Harris	Curatorial Assistant at Hertford Museum since 1985.
Ann Kirby	Trustee and one time Hertford Town Clerk
Edgar Lake	Friend, volunteer and long-time supporter of the Museum
James Nall-Cain	Architectural historian and volunteer at the Museum
Clive Partridge	Former Director of the Hart Archaeological Trust
Jean Purkis	Trustee and local historian
Alan White	Trustee and Chairman of the Friends of Hertford Museum

4 Hertford Museum Centenary

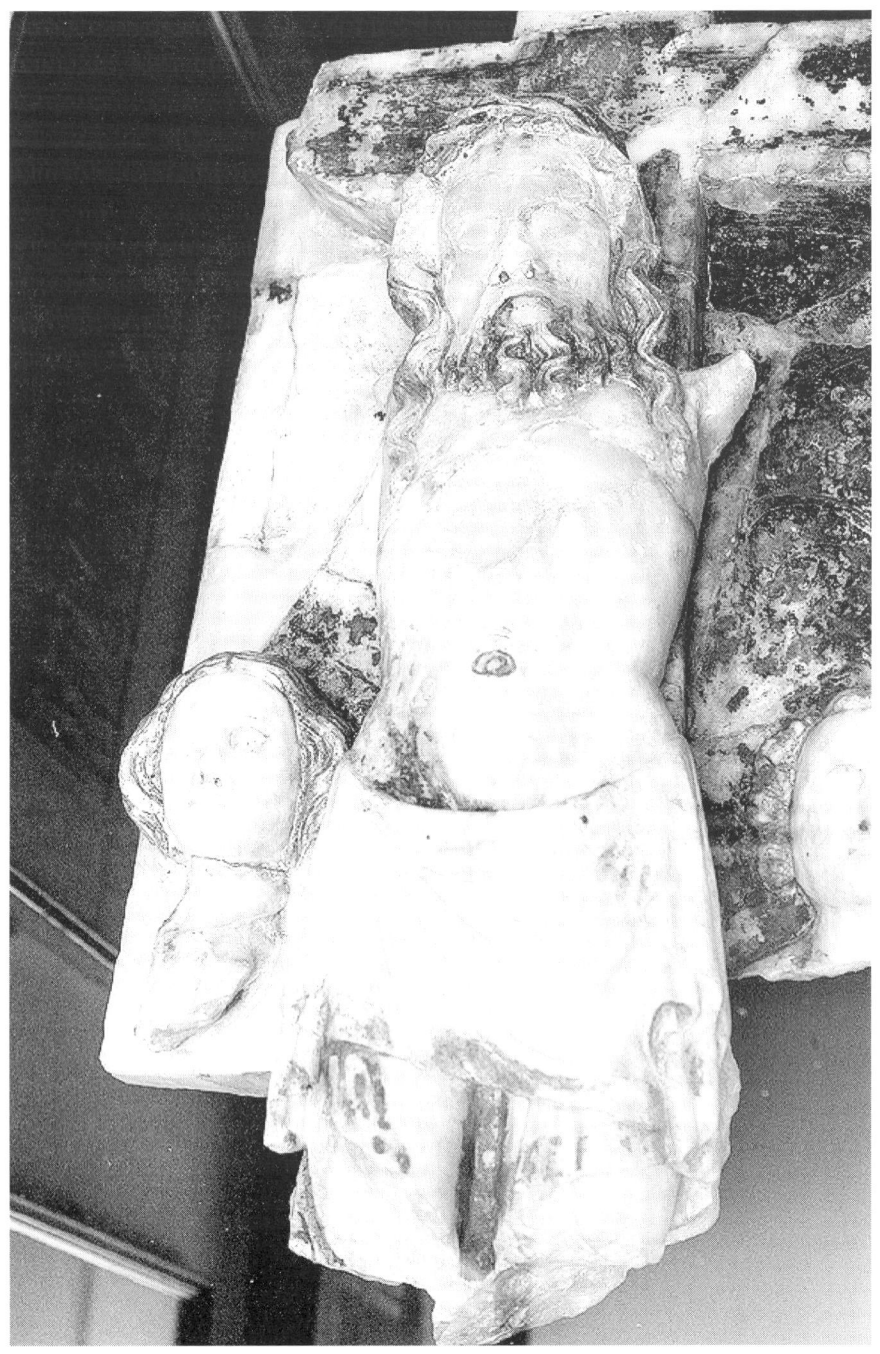

The alabaster crucifix from the ruined 14th century Church of St. Bartholomew, Layston, near Buntingford – Hertford Museum Collection (HETFM 4734.2.1-2). Photography courtesy of the Hertford Times.

PREFACE

The best local museums both reflect and enrich the communities in which they are set. Some are launched through the vision and determination of individuals to provide such a resource. In the case of Hertford Museum both these criteria apply. It was through the inspiration and flair of the Andrews brothers one hundred years ago in 1903 that Hertford Museum was established and it was through the continuing persistence of successive local authorities and trustee bodies that it has survived and flourished to celebrate the centenary which this book now commemorates.

The use of the pronoun "our" in the title emphasises the measure of community support which not only is represented in the number of contributors to this volume but also reveals the growing band of supporters, friends and volunteers who now enthusiastically launch the Museum into its second century. This is truly a collection of monographs and reminiscences which attempts to provide the reader with an account of the Museum's origins, setting, building, future plans and above all descriptions of the collections which remain at the heart of its contribution to the cultural and educational life of Hertford and beyond.

The first five chapters describe in some detail the Andrews family who established the Museum in 1903, something of the present building and its unique contribution to Hertford's architectural heritage and some of the more recent developments, particularly in relation to the Seed Warehouse. Jean Purkis and Edgar Lake reflect directly and through others on the setting of the Museum and some rather torrid periods in the forties.

The main sections describe in fascinating detail just some of the large collection of objects from far flung ethnographic through paper ephemera and militaria, to trade tokens, clocks and geology. The important chapter on archaeology emphasises the academic links between this science and the work of a collecting museum.

Prominence is given later in the book to the role being played by the Friends of the Museum. In recent years volunteers have become increasingly vital to the work of accessing and cataloguing the collections, and the year 2000 saw the setting up of the Patrons group; individuals committed to a certain annual gift to help stabilise the core funding of the Museum.

Finally, thanks must be expressed to the many donors of items and money to the Museum, but in the production of this centenary volume particular gratitude is due to the Hertford Civic Society for their most generous grant from the Melville Study Fund which made a reasonable print run possible.

Colin Harris
Chairman of Hertford Museum Trustees   July 2003

Chapter 1

THE ANDREWS FAMILY
by Rosemary Bennett

Hertford Museum first opened to the public, in October 1903, in the offices of its founders R.T. and W. F. Andrews, at 56 Fore Street (now No 98/100). It had been in the planning stage for a number of years as the museum's earliest accession register, dating from the 1880s, verifies. The driving force was Robert Thornton Andrews who poured a great deal of energy and a substantial amount of his personal wealth into the venture. He envisaged a free museum that local people would enjoy and one that would be worthy of the County Town. It must be remembered that this was long before the days of radio or television when the ordinary working man rarely travelled further than a nearby town. Robert wanted to bring the wonders of the world to the local people. Robert and his brother, William Frampton Andrews, are invariably known as R.T. and W.F. at the museum and that is how they will be referred to throughout this article. Both were members of the East Herts Archaeological Society founded in 1898.

The opening of the museum was announced in the local press and gifts and loans invited from the general public. All manner of items flooded in. There was no attempt to restrict or zone the type of item accepted, for the museum was virtually a giant "Cabinet of Curiosities". For a number of years W.F., three times Mayor of Hertford, fought for support from the Hertford Borough Council and it was the failure to achieve this, coupled with a determination not to relinquish a dream, that led to the purchase of 14 Bull Plain, in 1913. The premises, bought for £800 and the necessary alterations for its conversion to a museum, were entirely at the expense of the Andrews brothers and the museum was opened to the general public in February 1914. From the outset R.T. managed the practical and curatorial work. He was particularly interested in archaeology and enjoyed excavating when the opportunity arose. There is a photograph of him standing, spade in hand, in an excavation pit at Old Cross wearing a smart overcoat and bowler hat! It was taken when the remains of the church of St. Mary the Less were found when digging the foundation for the public library and was obviously a posed picture for the local press. He also built up an exceptionally fine collection of Hertfordshire trade tokens, which is by far the best in the county. W.F. concentrated on 'paper' items, such as books, maps, prints, drawings and a fascinating collection of general ephemera.

R.T. and W.F. Andrews were members of a very old established family that came

The interior of 56 Fore Street, showing the first museum display.

to Hertford in the 17th century. Thomas Andrews, his wife Ann and their son William, were the first to arrive here in the mid-17th century. They came from Plymouth and were devout puritans. At a time when many puritans were going west one wonders why this particular family came east to Hertford. As Plymouth was a Royalist town perhaps Thomas and his family left to follow Oliver Cromwell who was in the West Country before arriving in these parts in 1647. Thomas died in 1654 and was interred in the graveyard of All Saints' Church as indeed are a considerable number of his descendants. The son, William, was a builder and carpenter and became a Freeman of the Borough. He worked from the same Castle Street premises that were to remain in the family until 1967. Another William represents the third generation and, in addition to being a builder, this William also traded in timber. He became a Freeman in 1728 and died in 1767.

Abraham, a particularly strong character, represents the fourth generation. Commercialism on a large scale became a reality in Hertford when the new navigation cut, from opposite Ware Park Mill to Mill Bridge, was completed by 1772. This gradually led to the commercialisation of Folly Island into wharves and storage facilities. Abraham Andrews was among the first to rent "a plot" on Little Hartham from which he both exported and imported timber. Like his forbears he was a nonconformist. Abraham was a devout supporter of John Wesley, the founder of Methodism, who visited Hertford on several occasions. On his first visit Wesley preached from a platform erected over one of Abraham's sawpits, and after that in a schoolroom Abraham had built in the grounds of his Castle Street home. In one of his diaries, Wesley records the effect his words had on the young girls and adds "But how the scene was changed when I went to the boys! They seemed as dead as stones, and scarce appeared to mind anything that was said – nay some of them could hardly refrain from laughter. However I set in and explained to them the terrors of the Lord". Abraham also purchased a small cottage at East End Green, Hertingfordbury, for use as a meetinghouse. When John Wesley had a church built in London, Abraham ordered his carpenters to make a fine mahogany pulpit for it. The church, and Wesley's house which is next door, are now the Museum of Methodism and the pulpit can be seen there.

However, Abraham felt the need to do much more than make a gift of a pulpit – he was driven by missionary fervour to spread Wesley's beliefs. So, in 1792, Abraham handed the family business over to his son William and set sail for Norfolk, Virginia, on the SS 'Julia'. During the journey he made a will and it was not until it was proven did his family, back in Hertford, learn that he had died in 1802. They had heard nothing from him during the intervening years and one wonders what his wife and children thought of his actions. As they were members of the established church, perhaps the atmosphere in the home had lacked harmony.

In 1800, William Andrews was found dead on Waterford Marsh, with a shotgun by his side. Was he the victim of a tragic accident or did he commit suicide? That question will never be answered but his death meant the recall of his brother, Samuel, who had been working as a Government Clerk of Works on the erection of barracks at Plymouth and Maidstone. At this time France was in turmoil and the possibility of the French invading these shores was taken very seriously.

Samuel had his own ideas for expanding the family's business. He opened a brickfield near Bramfield, and established a dry dock, for building barges, on Folly Island. He operated barges on the navigation and like many other barge owners began trading in coal, which was much sought after in an area that was far away from a coalfield. As the Lee Navigation formed part of the coastal shipping network these barges were smaller versions of the Thames sailing barge and their russet coloured sails would have made a splendid sight. The Lee Navigation was part of the coastal shipping network and not the inland canal system worked by narrow boats. We know from the Andrews' papers that one of their barges was named "Prudence" and that it had been built in their own boatyard.

Samuel was also interested in agriculture. He had a farm at Rush Green, on the outskirts of Hertford, and another near Bramfield. However, the end of the Napoleonic Wars heralded a long period of agricultural depression and Samuel was forced to call a meeting of his creditors to request their continued support during the crisis. He pledged repayment with interest and on March 26, 1822 there appeared the following notice in the *County Chronicle*:

> Samuel Andrews begs leave to return his most grateful thanks to his friends and the public in general for the favours they have conferred upon him in the building, timber and coal business by whose assistance he has been enabled to meet the

difficulties his connections with agriculture occasioned ... any old accounts (or others) to Christmas last, that have not been fully settled by him, may be immediately forwarded.

Samuel's timber business was obviously extensive for it is on record that twenty pairs of sawyers were employed. Walter Andrews, in his family history, mentions that his grandfather had two ships' figureheads bought from the Woolwich Docks adorning his work yard and that its gateposts were cannons stood up on end. Clearly, collecting old and unusual items was a family trait. Samuel relinquished the "plot on Little Hartham" for more commodious premises nearby. He retired in 1838 and handed the control of the business over to his son and namesake. He had prepared for this by purchasing another property in the town, 27 West Street, and there he died in 1841.

Like his father, Samuel expanded the family business which by now had been in existence for some 200 years. He opened another brickfield and acquired two additional wharves – another on Folly Island, formerly owned by Thomas Hill, and the Ayres' Priory Wharf on the opposite bank of the navigation, on the site of the ancient Hertford Priory. Both Hill and Ayres were timber merchants and presumably Samuel also purchased the businesses and trading goodwill. Hill is mentioned in the diary of the Bramfield farmer, John Carrington, who, when describing Hertford's celebration of the Battle of Trafalgar, records "The great timber stick came to Hertford – 16 horses 12 load of timber from Great Offley, bought by Hill of Hertford for 100gns twas said ... it stood on the carriage at the Bull Plain 3 months and a scaffell built and regoicing for the Nelson victory". Samuel was a considerate employer. He continued to pay his workmen when they were ill, helped out if they fell on hard times and contributed towards a child's education when it showed promise.

Samuel married Maria Thornton, the daughter of a lime and cement merchant, who lived in Lombard House at the end of Bull Plain. Maria was a remarkable young woman. Extremely intelligent with a lively enquiring mind, she had a wide range of interests that encompassed numismatics, archaeology, and geology in addition to the usual ladylike pursuits of music and painting. Samuel and Maria had twelve children in sixteen years and sadly Maria died when the last child was born and it too died shortly afterwards. Samuel, like his father, was interested in farming and he acquired Stockings Farm, at Little Berkhamsted, where his children spent their holidays romping in the woods and fields. Samuel remarried twice and on retirement, after handing the management of his affairs to his two elder sons, moved to the house his father had bought in West Street. He died in 1866, leaving the business to R.T. and W.F. and their siblings each received an inheritance sufficient to provide them with an income for the rest of their lives.

Presumably all the sons went to the Hertford Grammar School (now the Richard Hale School). The eldest son R.T., the primary force behind the founding of the museum, was an architect and surveyor in addition to being a partner in the family firm. He had a separate studio/office just inside the yard gates. R.T. had been articled to the Hertford architect, David Morgan, who died when his pupil was only nineteen. Samuel bought the practice for his son but it has to be said that his work lacks the distinctive simplicity of his master's. The *Mercury* office building in Fore Street is an example of David Morgan's work. W.F. was primarily a timber merchant. Both John and Samuel Percy trained to be doctors at London's famous St. Bartholomew's Hospital. Owing to ill health Samuel Percy spent some time in Australia and while there purchased a collection of ferns that were sent back home to the "family" museum. At the onset of World War I, with so many young doctors needed to look after the war wounded, Samuel Percy came out of retirement to care for the poor living in the London slums. Arthur became a solicitor and Thomas went to sea. Thomas was shipwrecked off

Robert Thornton Andrews in later life

Shanghai and later drowned when he fell from the ship's rigging. The youngest child, Walter, entered the Church and went, in the late 1870s, to serve as a missionary in Japan. He was later appointed the Bishop of Hokkaido, an island in North Japan, and his work there is reflected in the museum's oriental collection. Walter returned home in 1909 and thereafter moved around a number of parishes including those of Chichester and St. Leonards, on the South Coast. Perhaps it was Walter who collected the many bibles that are in the Museum's collections.

In the family history, Walter gives a brief description of the lives of the male members of his family but makes few references to his sisters, other than Louisa. After her father's death Louisa visited Walter in Japan. This was surely a daunting journey for an unaccompanied single woman to have undertaken. There she met, and in 1884 married, the Venerable Dr. John Batchelor, a renowned scholar of the Ainu people. The Ainu are the aboriginal people of Japan who were driven north to Hokkaido in the 4th century. The Ainu people and its language that is unrelated to any other fascinated Dr. Batchelor. It is estimated that there are some 16,000 Ainu still living on the island of Hokkaido today. Batchelor wrote books about them and compiled an Ainu-English dictionary. Unfortunately Louisa died in Japan and her husband, who had intended to end his days in the country he had come to love so much, was forced to return to England when World War II started. He was then over ninety and he too has left his mark on the museum's collections.

It was the New River Company's rebuilding of the bridge, linking Bull Plain to Folly Island, in 1860 that forced R.T. and W.F. to concentrate their business on the Priory Wharf site. The new bridge made it difficult to get long lengths of timber to their Folly Island wharves without damaging the bridge's high walls.

W.F. Andrews in his mayoral robes – he was three times Mayor of Hertford

This led to the brothers building houses on the sites of their two wharves. They then negotiated to buy the remainder of Folly Island, except for the Hertford Corporation's "Little Hartham", from the Balls Park Estate. The first street to be developed was "The Folly" in 1866, and the last was Frampton Street in 1893. The houses were unpretentious homes for the working-class family and were designed by R.T. and built by the family firm. Ownership of the cottages was divided between them and after the death of W.F., in 1916, his were gradually sold but R.T.'s descendants retained their interest until the 1990s, when two deaths in the family, within a short space of time, resulted in the crippling double payment of inheritance tax.

Papers in the museum's collections reveal the extent of the Andrews brothers' property holdings. They were responsible for a number of quite extensive estates including one at Waltham Cross and another at Southall in Middlesex. Nearer to home are houses at St. Albans. In addition R.T. and W.F. bought up assorted groups of cottages in hamlets and villages around Hertford.

After their retirement R.T. and W.F. Andrews continued to administer their properties and act as insurance agents from their Fore Street address. After William's death in 1916 the Fore Street Office was closed and Robert continued to work as an architect and insurance agent from a small office in Church Street. Like most prominent Hertford businessmen R.T. was active in local affairs. He was for many years a member of the Board of Guardians for the County Hospital and served in the same capacity for the workhouse. R.T was proud of The Folly estate and it is said that when collecting rents, he always had a duster in his pocket to eradicate any graffiti.

Walter Andrews, in his family history, writes that W.F., although he looked taciturn was a generous and caring man. Like his father he had contributed to school fees, including those of Walter's son and the sons of his workforce. W.F. was a sidesman at All Saints' Church for twenty-two years and after the disastrous fire which resulted in the present church having to be built, William pledged a £100 every year until the rebuilding was completed. He paid for the replacement of bell no. 7. He donated the beautiful carved alabaster altar screen in memory of his wife, Susan, and paid for the replacement of one of the bells as all of them had melted and could only be sold for scrap metal. W. F. also provided the land needed for both the St. John's Hall and the Mission Hall (now the Pioneer Hall) in the Ware Road.

When Robert Andrews died in 1926 supervision of the museum passed to his son Herbert, who was the Librarian of the Victoria and Albert Museum. Herbert lived in Dulwich and he appointed Henry Robins to look after the day-to-day functioning of the museum. Robins had been proprietor of the Dicker Mills until he was overtaken by financial disaster in 1924. He was an avid collector with a wide range of interests and was a very good musician. He gave the museum a number of beautifully illuminated ancient Hertfordshire manor rolls and also memorabilia connected with Thomas Green and Charles Bridgeman, whose successive tenures of the post of organist at All Saints' Church covered much of the 18th and 19th centuries.

During Word War II Herbert and his family moved to the comparative peace of Hertford and lived temporarily on the museum premises, in rooms that have been rebuilt as office and staff accommodation. It was Herbert who reopened negotiations with the Hertford Borough Council to take over the museum after his "tenure". This took the form of the Borough Council paying the staff wages while all other expenses were met by income generated by a trust fund established by the Andrews family. At first the museum became the responsibility of the Borough Librarian which was not an unusual arrangement at the time. However, a report, commissioned by the Government in 1963, recommended that this practice should cease and that all museums should be under the day-to-day management of a curator. This resulted in the appointment of the first of Hertford Museum's qualified curators. It is very pleasing that members of the Andrews family, particularly Herbert's three grandsons, still take an active interest in the museum founded by their forbears.

The Andrews Family   13

The four Andrews brothers, photographed in the garden of 25 Castle Street in about 1906. Left to right: William Frampton, Dr. Samuel Percy, Robert Thornton and the Right Revd. Walter Andrews who had been Bishop of Hokkaido in Japan.

Chapter 2

A HISTORY OF THE BUILDING AND GARDEN
by James Nall-Cain

The history of the Museum is linked to two buildings: 54-56 Fore Street, where it was created and 18 Bull Plain, which is its present location. The Museum started in 1903 and the collection was moved to Bull Plain in 1914. The history and restoration of the Bull Plain garden are directly connected to the Museum.

The contemporary photograph opposite (Plate 1) by Sneesby from the Museum collection shows 54-56 Fore Street (now 98-100 Fore Street) when it was Robert Thornton's and William Frampton Andrews' business premises. The building still stands, although partly rebuilt, and is now occupied by Saks.

The ground floor shop windows had been put in by E.J. Harvey in 1902[1] and they still exist to this day. However, the first floor and gables were rebuilt in 1932 with a Mansard style roof and cornice by Prudential Assurance.

I feel that the present red brick building may have had an earlier structure beneath. Norden's survey of 1621[2] describes it as "… one ancient messuage called the Stone House and one yard, one garden or orchard adjoining … sold unto Richard Hale … did erect a free school …" This building therefore was possibly the site of Hale's Grammar School built in 1617.

A.J. Wenham, Adkins and a tailor called Reeves[3] later occupied the site. Its next incarnation was as the Post Office from 1859 to 1891. The Andrews brothers bought the building on the 25th of March 1891.

No. 54 is described in a sales particular[4] of the 11th of August 1900, as being occupied by the Master of Hales' Grammar School as a Boarding House and Residence. It was built of brick and timber and had four reception rooms and eight bedrooms.

On October 6th 1903 R.T. and W.F. Andrews announced in a letter to the *Hertfordshire Mercury* that the Museum "is now open, and is free to visitors from 2.30 to 4.30 p.m. on every weekday except Thursday until further notice."

A Museum room was created in 1903 and it was extended to two further rooms by 1909. In 1913 the brothers purchased 18 Bull Plain for £800 and the Museum reopened there on February 26th 1914.

18 Bull Plain (Plate 2, on page 16) dates from circa 1610. No. 20 next door takes its name, Tooke House, from the builders of the block, Mary and William Tooke. They lived in Lombard House, the old jettied building by the river, now the Hertford

The Building and Garden 15

*Plate 1: Front elevation of 54-56 Fore Street, by Sneesby
(Hertford Museum collection HETFM: 6205.155)*

16   Hertford Museum Centenary

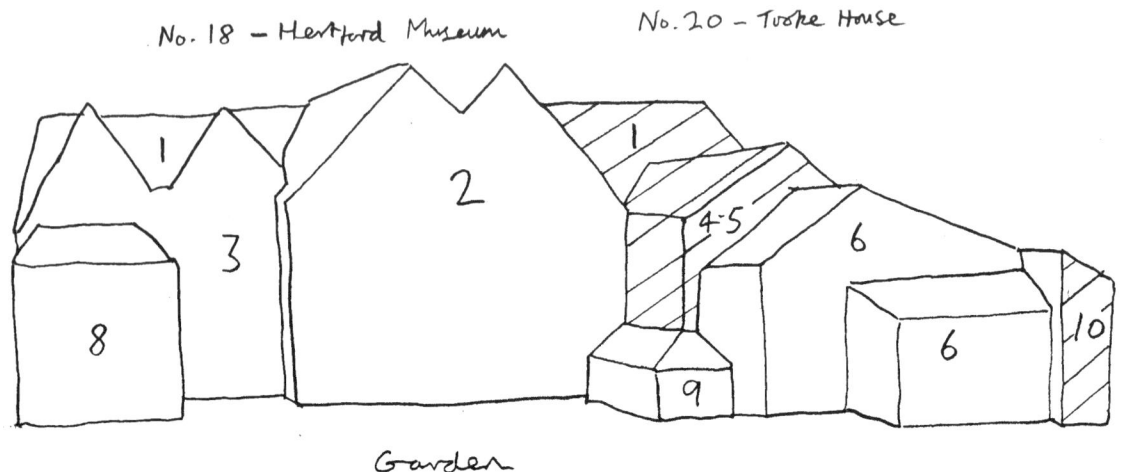

Plate 2: 18-20 Bull Plain in 1914, by Elsden (Hertford Museum collection HETFM: 6236.140)
Below, Figure 1: Building History of 18-20 Bull Plain, sketch of rear elevation (after A.G. Davies)

Club. The famous Hertfordshire historian, Sir Henry Chauncy (died 1700) later lived in the house.

In Norden's survey[5] the building is described thus:

"Mary Tooke, widow aforesaid holdeth for life one cottage newly erected going to Butcherley Green …" (now the Bircherley Green Shopping Centre) "divided into two, yearly rent 4d."

William, her late husband, was the Bailiff (roughly equivalent to the modern Mayor) of Hertford in 1577. He died in 1611.

However the Museum does not appear on John Speede's map of 1611.

The original Bull Plain façade is a four bay post and truss building (no.1 on Figure 1 opposite).

Internally very little remains from this period except probably the upper flight of stairs leading to the attic and much of the roof rafters and exposed beams. This oak staircase (Plate 3, below) has plain newels with ball finials and barley-sugar twist columns. One of the exposed beams of the first floor has a chamfer and double tongue.

Plate 3: Staircase to the attic at 18 Bull Plain, (kindly reproduced by permission of English Heritage, the National Monuments Record)

The roof has halved and pegged rafters with butt perlins, as does the roof at Lombard House. There are also jettied eaves. No. 20 has a similar staircase and roof timbers. It probably also had a gabled outshoot.

In circa 1640-1660 (No.2 on Figure 1) the timber-framed building was clad in brick and a southern wing was built to the rear. The wall plates were butted against those of the original building, and tenoned purlins with upper and lower common rafters were once again adopted. A broken brick was found to contain the bowl of a clay pipe of circa 1640-1660[7]. In circa 1660-1685 (No.3 on Figure 1) another wing was built to the rear of the building.

This staircase wing is shown by the two gables as No.3 on Figure 1. A stairwell was built in the space between the southern and central wings, probably replacing an earlier one. Here the roof consists of vertical posts held by plates supporting the rafters.

In the mid 18th century the front elevation on Bull Plain was "refronted" with new sash windows, a common fate meted out to 17th century buildings in the town.

On the ground floor, there is a beautiful early 19th century shop window with a Tuscan pilaster surround, entablature with plain frieze and a moulded cornice. This is matched to the left of the door by a replica of circa 1950.

There is a fanlight above the Museum doorway with tracery of half and quarter circles. This is set in a very fine early 19th century door case with reeded Tuscan pilasters and a slim moulded cornice hood.

In the 19th and 20th centuries the rear of the building went through a rather confusing phase. A staircase wing was added to no. 20 in two phases (Nos.4 & 5 on Figure 1). A Victorian rear extension was built (No.6 on Figure 1) which was to be used as the Museum offices from 1914 to 1988. This is clearly shown to the right on Plate 4. It was demolished and replaced by the modern offices comprising two toilets, an administrator's office, kitchen, library and curator's office.

In 1884 the Mission Hall (later renamed Oddfellows Hall) was added to No. 20 (No.7 on Figure 1). This is shown on the left of the Bull Plain frontage in Plates 1 and 4. An outshoot was also added in 1898 (No.10 on Figure 1). In 1881-1898 the staircase wing to the Museum was enlarged (No.8 on Figure 1). This is clearly shown to the left of the Museum building in Plate 4. Finally, a corridor was built joining the former back offices to the Museum in 1903-1913 (No.9 on Figure 1).

The entire Museum building was opened out removing the internal walls. The Mayor officially opened the Museum at 3 p.m on Thursday 26th February 1914, and this ceremony was followed by Tea at 3.45 p.m.

A contemporary news cutting describes the alterations thus: "The old house, which had 15 rooms, has been divested of its internal walls and chimney stacks, and iron girders and columns have been put in their places, so that there are now three spacious rooms, one on each floor. The whole of the back windows have been enlarged and others added in front so as to admit the greatest amount of light … the painting

The Building and Garden

is white throughout … the contract for the alteration was carried out by Messrs Ginn and Son, under the supervision of Messrs. Andrews surveyor, Mr. Andrew Gray …"

The Museum remains much the same today.

The Garden

The original Jacobean garden, it has been surmised[12], probably stretched back to Green Street and was rectangular in shape, 170 feet long by 90 feet wide. It may have had a pair of knot gardens close to the house, a willow arbour, turf seat, balustrade, bee-house and fruit trees around the wall. There might have been a pleasure garden near the house with an orchard and kitchen garden beyond, surrounded by a hawthorn hedge, wicket, fence or wall.

No.18 retained the garden area when the house was divided up. On an 1893 plan, the garden is shown with steps leading up to it. The end of the original garden has been built on but it is otherwise largely intact. There are areas of lawn with flower borders on two sides and what could be fruit trees.

By 1913 it was described thus "… large garden with lawn, summerhouse, kitchen garden, well-stocked with fruit trees, asparagus bed, etc., two poultry houses …" At some stage the brick wall we see today was put up running Northwest–Southeast, probably after the Museum sold part of the garden in 1980.

In 1988, the decision was made to transform the small garden behind the Museum, into a Jacobean Knot garden. This would complement and enhance the building and provide an outdoor extension to the museum.

The new garden contains plants and features typical of a garden of the period

Plate 4: Rear of the Museum showing car park, c. 1960s
(Hertford Museum Collection HETFM 6205.230)

1610-1625. In the course of the rebuilding of the garden, a pillar-box and a stone coffin were unearthed and moved to the Museum. Dr. Diana Kingham of Glorious Gardens drew up a planting plan for the garden.

The knot design chosen for the garden was one based on a heraldic device from a design published by Thomas Hill in 1577. The hedges were planted with lavender, germander and box. Gravel, coal and crushed brick were used as coloured infill. The Jacobean plants used included Thyme, Jacob's ladder, Carnations, Foxglove, Wormwood and Tansy. A Camomile Seat, Arbour and Bee Skep were made and a fruit tree trained up the wall. The whole design is intended to be viewed from above and the garden looks wonderful from the upper floors of the Museum.

The new garden was opened on Saturday 11th May 1991, and it received a Civic Society Award that same year.

The building is constantly evolving, with the recent

Plate 5: Rear of Museum (Hertford Museum Collection No. 33951)

Plate 6: Hertford Museum Garden in July 1991.

additions of the new shop and the latest galleries. The buildings and the garden have served the Museum well in the hundred years since its inception!

NOTES

1   R.T. Andrews Gazetteer p.25 (Hertford Museum)
2   Transcription of John Norden's Survey of 1621, p.74 no.5 (Hertford Museum)
3   R.T. Andrews Gazetteer p.25 (Hertford Museum)
4   Sales particular Norris & Duvall, 11th August 1900 (HETFM: 3806-140)
5   Norden Survey of 1621 p.101 no. 76 (Hertford Museum)
6   18-20 Bull Plain, Notes by A.G. Davies, January 1987 (Hertford Museum)
7   R.T. Andrews Gazetteer p.156 (Hertford Museum)
8   Dr. Diana Kingham's Notes (Hertford Museum)
9   Sales particular Braund & Oram, 22nd February 1913 (HETFM: 3806-51)

Glossary

Ball Finial	Top of a newel
Bay	A vertical division marked by windows or roof compartments on a façade
Butt perlins	Piece of timber tenoned into either side of the principal timbers
Cornice	Projecting decorative feature along the top of a wall
Entablature	Part above a column. It comprises the architrave, the frieze and the cornice
Exposed beams	Timber beams that are visible
Façade	The front of a building
Fanlight	A window, often semi-circular, over a door. The glazingbars are usually in a fan shape
Frieze	Middle part of an entablature
Gable	The triangular upper part of a wall at the end of a pitched roof
Jettied	The projection of an upper storey beyond the storey below
Mansard sroof	Roof with a double slope, the lower being longer and steeper than the upper
Newel	The principal post where a flight of stairs meets a landing
Outshoot	Timber framed extension jutting out from the main building
Pilaster	A rectangular column projecting only slightly from the wall
Post & truss building	Building comprising vertical posts between trusses
Roof rafters	Roof timbers sloping up from the wall-plate to the ridge
Weatherboarded	A wall covered with overlapping boards of timbers

Chapter 3

THE DEVELOPMENT OF THE MUSEUM
by Ann Kirby

Up to the early 1980s the Museum buildings had seen little change since the Andrews brothers had arranged their collections at 18 Bull Plain in 1913/14. Long term residents of Hertford remember with nostalgia the familiar exhibits: the suit of Japanese armour, the model of the Shire Hall, the two-headed chicken. Short of both financial and staffing resources, the Museum was simply ticking over. Some academic research was being carried out, some special exhibitions were arranged but the Museum had little impact on the town and visitor numbers were low.

Changes were planned for the Hertford Town Centre in the late 1970s. A "space-age shopping centre" was proposed in one large block from Bull Plain to the present bus station. The Museum itself, as a listed building, was safe but it owned an important piece of land (behind the present garden) which was part of the proposed site. This was eventually sold in 1980 for £125,000 which provided a Capital Trust Fund and a useful annual income. Both of these come under Charity Commission regulations and none of the capital can be spent without the specific approval of the Charity Commission.

Fortunately the newly formed Hertford Civic Society managed to resist the "space-age" development and save the buildings of Bull Plain and round the corner into Railway Street. The buildings which were erected were more in keeping with the existing town.

In the early 1980s the elements took a hand – the Museum roof began to leak badly. The Architects' Department of Hertfordshire County Council was asked to supervise the work of replacing the roof, which involved repairing and replacing beams and re-tiling. All of this had to be in keeping with the listed building which is an important feature in the conservation area. Fortunately, because of the building's status, grants were available from the Department of the Environment and others to help pay for the repairs.

But before the roof repairs could begin the attic space had to be cleared and it was full of boxes containing the finds from archaeological digs all over the area. The boxes were piled up high and there was only a narrow pathway allowing people to edge sideways around the mountains. All these boxes had to be removed to the Museum Stores at the Seed Warehouse – an enormous task. The attic floor beams were then found to be somewhat deflected by the weight of the archaeological finds.

The repairs to the roof were completed by early 1984 and later in that year the exterior of the Museum was redecorated. Not only was the fabric of the Museum receiving attention but also attempts were being made to encourage public interest. In 1982 the "Friends of Hertford Museum" organisation was founded. Its aims were to support the Museum and its work "by raising money, getting publicity, providing practical help with the Museum's work and generally doing our best to increase public awareness." Although numbers of Friends have not been large over the years, the organisation has tried to fulfil its aims and has certainly drawn in a number of very willing and helpful supporters for the Museum.

1985 saw redecoration of the ground floor display area and new floor covering for the same space. The Nunn Key sign, damaged by a high lorry, was restored at Ware College through the sponsorship of the members of the Chamber of Commerce.

The appointment of Rosemary Bennett as Curator for Collections in July 1985 was an important increase in qualified personnel at the Museum. Rosemary's very valuable contribution over the years to the knowledge of local History in Hertford is rightly acclaimed.

Hertfordshire County Council appointed its first Museums Development Officer in the early 1980s and from 1979 the Standing Committee for Museums in Hertfordshire began to hold regular meetings at which representatives included professional staff, Trustees and Councillors. The Director of the Area Museum Service for South East England (AMSSEE), Crispin Paine, also attended these meetings as did the Clerk to the Trustees of Hertford Museum, who took the opportunity to discuss the needs of the Hertford Museum with these officers and began to receive help and advice. A meeting was arranged with the County and District Councils. AMSSEE also agreed to help.

In the meantime, professional reports on the Geology collections, on light conditions and on security were obtained through AMSSEE and the Trustees were persuaded that the rear wing of the Museum should be demolished and rebuilt.

The original rear building consisted of a kitchen/office on the ground floor, a very steep and narrow staircase to one upper room with low head height in the middle and sloping roofs, with even lower head heights, at each side. There were also some tumbledown outhouses containing some of the Museum's extensive collection of mangles. At that time the Curator's office occupied about half of the present Special Exhibition area downstairs and it was partitioned off from the display area. The office was dominated by a large table piled with books and objects.

The Charity Commission agreed to release some of the Museum's capital funds for the rebuilding work on condition that annual repayments were made in order to replenish the Capital Trust Fund. The work was extended to include the building of a fireproof screen around the main staircase and the installation of a metal stair from the first landing to the garden as a fire escape. There was an official reopening on 29th April 1988 for the new rear wing which now had two useful rooms on each floor and a modern lavatory for the staff.

Before work began on the rear wing, a new member of staff had joined the Museum. Sarah Gray was the first Director of the Museum (later known as the Senior Curator). She served from 1st June 1987 to 31st March 1991 and AMSSEE, HCC and East Hertfordshire District Council (EHDC) all gave financial support to her appointment and salary.

Although the plans for the new rear wing were already well in hand before Sarah's arrival, her talents and energy were soon turned to other projects. AMSSEE had offered a special grant of £15,000 towards specific items such as environmental protection for the displays.

Hertford Museum is fortunate in the wealth of its collections, some of national importance, but like many other Museums it has always had problems in displaying as many objects as possible and providing suitable storage for the reserve collections. Even in the time of the Andrews brothers one can imagine that their house in Castle Street and their office at 56 Fore Street were stuffed with the treasures they had accumulated over the years. The move to more commodious premises at Bull Plain must have been a great relief, but even this building was unable to contain the reserve collections by the 1970s.

It was the ambitious plans to celebrate the 13th Centenary of the Synod of Hertford (673 AD) in 1973 that stimulated Hertford Borough Council to purchase the old McMullen's Seed Warehouse in Maidenhead Yard in 1972. The Council was soon to become a "successor Town Council" after the abolition of Hertford Borough Council following the Local Government Reorganisation of 1972 but the Borough Council entered into the spirit of the Synod Summer.

An exhibition space was badly needed for the many displays which took place during that summer and the area at the front of the Seed Warehouse provided this space. The rest of the building remained as it had been, dusty and unrestored with low ceilings and poor access to the upper floors.

Eventually the possibility of storing the Museum's reserve collections in the Seed Warehouse was agreed but, once again, lack of finance and shortage of staff meant that the objects were not carefully stored and recorded. The removal of the boxes of archaeological finds from the Museum attic to the Seed Warehouse at the time of the roof repairs has already been noted. The removal of the Roman corndryer from Foxholes Farm to the Seed Warehouse in 1977 is dealt with in Chapter 10.

After the Synod, some use continued to be made of the exhibition/meeting space in the Seed Warehouse and in the mid 1980s the Town Council paid for a complete refurbishment of this area. It was re-opened as "The Mill Bridge Rooms" in April 1988 but the museum stores in the rest of the building remained in very poor condition.

Around 1987/88 the Hertfordshire Archaeological Trust was looking for new premises, having outgrown both its office space on the opposite side of Bull Plain to the Museum and other storage/workshop premises elsewhere. The then Director of the Museum, Sarah Gray, and the Clerk of the Museum Trustees made an investigative

The Development of the Museum 25

'The Seed Warehouse' – a watercolour by Nick Jones, 1990, purchased by the Hertford Museum in the same year and now in the Collection: HEFTM: 1990.13.1

tour of the Seed Warehouse and then sat down to discuss the possibilities. With rising excitement the group realised the great potential of the building as a centre for heritage related activities and plotted how this could be achieved.

Proposals for the refurbishment of the whole building were eventually accepted by Hertford Town Council which funded the major part of the work through Public Works Loan Board loans (paid off over 10½ years). A grant of £15,000 was received from the Museums and Galleries Commission. The County and District Councils and the Historic Buildings and Monuments Commission as well as the Hertfordshire Archaeological Trust all contributed to the costs.

In order to carry out this major work, the whole building had to be cleared – another mammoth task for the museum staff. In this they were assisted by a band of dedicated volunteers from the East Hertfordshire Decorative and Fine Arts Society (EHDFAS). Everything was wrapped up, packed in boxes and transported to a dry and secure barn in the Hertford countryside where it remained safely while the builders were at work.

The return of these reserve collections to the refurbished Seed Warehouse was possibly an even bigger task. By then, special storage racks had been purchased and fitted into the Small Objects Store. The smaller items were unpacked with the help of the EHDFAS volunteers before taking their places in an orderly manner in an environmentally controlled area where temperature and humidity are kept at appropriate levels. The opportunity was also taken to record many of the objects for the Museum's database.

Plans were made for the official re-opening of the Seed Warehouse in November 1989. It was hoped that the local government and heritage minister, Virginia Bottomley MP, would declare the building open but a Cabinet re-shuffle moved her to a less appropriate Ministry. Fortunately work had not begun on the commemorative plaque so the name of Patrick Cormack MP was quickly substituted and on 6th November he made an excellent speech and cut the ribbon in fine style.

In 1989 more staff changes took place. Early in the year Gordon Davies departed from the Museum after almost 25 years of loyal service, originally as Curator and later as Curator (Research). Later that year Sheila Every was appointed as the Museum's first Administrative Officer. Another first was the appointment of Simon Townsend by East Herts District Council as the first East Herts District Curator, based at Hertford Museum but with responsibilities for other small museums in the District.

The Museum Garden was in a sorry state after the rebuilding of the rear wing. The storage of building materials had destroyed the former rather natural and romantic arrangement. It was decided that a Jacobean Garden to match the period of the Museum building would be appropriate and a Knot Garden design was prepared by Dr. Diana Kingham. Box cuttings were obtained from Hatfield House and Van Hage's Garden Centre sponsored much of the planting. Toilet facilities for the public were also built on one side of the garden (the first time the Museum had been able to offer such a facility). The rough wooden poles supporting the roof of the pergola were made from the trunks of the large evergreen trees which had shaded the old Museum Garden. Mrs. Theodora Van Hage performed the opening ceremony of the garden on 11th May 1991. There was a Knot garden cake and Ida Coyston made a Knot Garden tapestry.

Later in 1991 the Museum's Jacobean Garden received an Award from Hertford Civic Society and the Seed Warehouse refurbishment was Highly Commended by the same judges.

Patrick Cormack MP and Councillor Peter Ruffles, Deputy Mayor, at the official reopening of the Seed Warehouse in November 1989. (Reproduced by kind permission of Archaeological Solutions – previously known as the Hertfordshire Archaeological Trust).

The first issue of Hertford Museum News for the period April to September 1989 brought history, news and information about exhibitions and the activities of the Friends in a lively format. The Newsletter still continues to appear at regular intervals. It is distributed to Friends, schools and libraries and is freely available at the Museum. It is most valuable in attracting visitors.

Redisplay of the ground floor of the Museum was also being considered. Designers presented plans for a new window display and for a Hertfordshire Gallery which was intended to showcase some of the Museum's greatest treasures. Some of the early designs included part of the first floor and there were amazing proposals for book-shaped cases which were eventually discarded. Hertfordshire County Council generously agreed to fund the Hertfordshire Gallery and the splendid cases were constructed to show treasures such as the Sawbridgeworth Helms, the Rowlandson watercolour of the Bell Inn at Hertford and special archaeological finds. The work included the grading of the floor to remove a large step up from the front to the back of the building. Redecoration took place and new floor covering was laid. The front section of the south wing was redisplayed in 1992 as an "Early Days" exhibition, showing an area as it would have been at the time of the Andrews Brothers. The Hertfordshire Gallery was eventually opened by the Chairman of the County Council in 1993.

Having instigated both the Knot Garden project and the Hertfordshire Gallery project, it was sad that Sarah Gray left the Museum on 31st March 1991 before they were completed. It was good that she came back to the opening ceremonies for both. Without her energy, determination and sheer hard work over the four years of her service the major improvements to the buildings and collections could not have taken place.

It was appropriate that Dr. Diana Kingham, who had designed the Knot Garden, was Acting Curator during the period when the garden was being completed.

Andrea George became Senior Curator from 3rd June 1991 and presided over further repairs and improvements as well as exciting exhibitions before she left the Museum at the end of March 2002.

Work continued behind the scenes at the Museum. The attics, no longer filled with archaeological finds, were provided with racks for the Museum's fascinating collection of election posters and other paper treasures. There were concerns about woodworm attack and rot in the attic and first floor. Some of it was damage due to the long term effects of leaks from the roof. Timber treatment was carried out and floors repaired and strengthened during 1992. The Town Centre Conservation Fund made a grant towards this.

A prominent member of the Old Hertfordians proposed that in 1993 Hertford should celebrate the centenary of the birth of Captain W.E. Johns (author of the Biggles and Worrals books). This was taken up enthusiastically by the new Senior Curator, Andrea George, who contacted local relatives of Captain Johns, authors of books about him and the club "Biggles and Co." which had members in many countries. The resulting exhibition in 1993 "Biggles Comes Home to Hertford" produced record visitor figures including many foreign visitors (a group from Holland came to the Opening Ceremony.) There was a celebration meal at the Old Hertfordians Club and another at the RAF Club in Piccadilly as well as a showing of the Biggles film at the National Film Theatre and a special "Biggles Flies Again" day at the Shuttleworth Collection, Old Warden. A truly exciting year!

In 1994 the Robert Kiln Charitable Trust funded the refurbishment of the Activity Room on the first floor, aimed particularly at use by children. The room was decorated, carpeted and provided with suitable tables and chairs. This room has been very well used over the succeeding years for meetings of the Friends of the Museum, meetings of volunteers and especially for children's activities at half-term holidays and on Medieval Night. To see the room full of busy children and parents making shields or dinosaurs, drawing, colouring, cutting out, making splendid friezes for the walls, is to see young people becoming interested in the Museum and what goes on there – a good omen for the future.

So, over the last twenty years the Museum has seen major improvement to all its buildings, its storage and its displays. Only the first floor remains to be redisplayed. It is to be hoped that grants can be obtained to carry out this project during the first years of Hertford Museum's second century. This is a project for the Centenary Appeal.

Over the same period there have been significant additions to the Museum's collections, thanks to donations by the public, the Friends of the Museum, local businesses and the National Art Collection Fund administered by the Victoria and Albert Museum. These included

— the Rowlandson watercolours – the Bell Inn at Hertford purchased in 1984 and the Bull Inn at Hertford purchased 1988
— the Hertfordshire Wagon 1988
— the Anglo Saxon Silver Penny 1989
— the Much Hadham Coin Hoard 1991
— the Bronze Age Sword and Palstave 1991

All these received publicity in the Local Press and drew people to visit the Museum to see them. Good relations with the *Hertfordshire Mercury* have resulted in many reports and photographs of Museum activities. These have encouraged members of the public to visit the Museum and enjoy the special exhibitions and events as well as the permanent displays.

From 29th September 1998 to March 1999 the Museum held an exhibition "Pans and Polish – Cooking and Cleaning in Victorian times". In conjunction with this, after two years of consultation with teachers and educationalists, a professionally produced Education Resource Pack for Schools was made available. It was structured around the work of a servant girl called Millie and focused on four areas: cooking, cleaning, washing and lighting. This attracted visits from schools around the county thanks to preparation and hard work by Andrea George.

National recognition was also accorded to Hertford Museum when the Arts Minister, Alan Howarth MP, cited this resource pack as an example of good practice in his opening speech to a National Conference "Museums and the Learning Age" in London in July 1999.

Chapter 4

BULL PLAIN: A BRIEF HISTORY AND MEMORIES
by Jean Purkis

A 'Plain' in former times meant a wide-open space surrounded by buildings. Bull Plain is an example. It was described by John Norden in his 1620 survey as 'the way leadinge towards Little Hartham' across the water: the tip of today's Folly Island – with access by wooden footbridge.

In 1620 six properties were recorded in the street. As one entered from modern Salisbury Square, on the right or east was Christopher White's house and garden; next, to the north, was Elizabeth White's house, divided into two. Then came a cottage 'newly erected' and backing on to Butcherie Green, also divided: today's Tooke House and Hertford Museum. This belonged to Mary Tooke as did the imposing house abutting the Licker Mill Stream, now the Lea Navigation – Lombard (often corrupted to Lumber) House, presently the Hertford Club. In Henry VI's time it was called Malloreys, possibly after its first owner, circa 1442. Another, John Lombard, died in 1487. In the 1680s, Henry Chauncy, a JP and later county historian, stayed at Lombard House. On the west side was the house later called 'Waterside', owned by John Sharley or Shirley. This important property was severely damaged in the Zeppelin raid of 1915, which necessitated its demolition. The clinic stands on part of its site.

A pen and ink wash drawing of 'Waterside' in 1800 – artist unknown.

*Thomas Rowlandson: the Bull Inn 1800, from a watercolour
(Hertford Museum Collection HETFM: 1988.32.1)*

Last was an extensive coaching inn, the Prince's Arms, stretching from Hertford Cameras to the corner of Maidenhead Street, incidentally adjoining another inn on the site of Edinburgh Woollen Mills, called the Glove and Dolphin. After the Civil War in the mid 17th Century the Prince's Arms became the Bull.

In the early 18th Century a distinctive property emerged: today's No.16 – Beadle House. Evidence found in 1946 and 1955 by members of East Herts Archaeological Society (EHAS) suggested that it was an older property largely rebuilt. In 1703-4 it was sold unfinished by Sarah Crowch to Alderman John Dimsdale. The site previously accommodated three cottages bought by Sarah in 1701 from Walter Dickenson, perhaps converted from part of Elizabeth White's houses or built in her garden. Lombard House, owned by Robert Keynton, provided lodgings for Assize Judges. Waterside was contemporarily described as old, 'with a hall in the centre opening on to a small square court in which were also entrances to the dining-room and kitchen'. This description, unearthed by R.T. Andrews, accords with the drawing of 1800. The garden, which extended down to the water, was later to provide the site for cottages, still in existence. The occupier was John Pryor, woolstapler, who in 1757 married Mary Bray, daughter of Andrew, from whom Bray's Folly (one early name for Folly Island) is derived. A Miss Tyler was owner in the late 19th Century – a descendant of John Pryor. The footbridge was replaced in 1738 by 'Folly Bridge' for wheeled traffic.

By the 19th Century cottages, shops and worksheds had infilled the gardens of the big houses as businesses. In 1862, for example, there were: James Pamphilon, plumber; John Price, lodging house; Thomas Taylor, engineer & ironmonger; Fanny Ward, toy and fancy dealer; Imperial Fire & Pelican Life Assurance companies; Literary & Scientific Institute – now John Marchant; J.F. Lyon, solicitor; G. Brodie, clocks & watches; Alfred Green, boots & shoes; Eliza Hackney, straw bonnets; John Kitchen, cowkeeper, Waterside; Richard Medcalf, coach-builder.

The Bull Inn was flourishing in 1832, the 'Zephir' coach departing for London six days a week at 7.30 am and the 'Express' to Hull and Lincoln at 6.30 pm. From 1848 for about 10 years, Catholic Mass was celebrated in a theatre attached to the Inn, before the church was built in St. John Street. In 1863, with the decline of coach travel, the inn was demolished leaving only the 'tap' to continue as the 'Bull' (now In Depth and Hertford Cameras). The site was rebuilt with shops and living accommodation. John Carrington, Bramfield farmer-diarist records:

> October ... 1805 The 22, the Great Timber Stick came to Hartford, 16 horses, 12 Load of Timber from Great Offley, Bought by Hill of Hertford for 100 Guineas as twas said ... and it stood on the carriage at the Bull plane 3 Months & a Scaffil built & Rejoyceings for Nelson's Victtory. Hill lived on the Bull Plane.

He did, he is in Holden's Annual directory, 1811: Robert Hill, Timber Merchant.

Early in the century Amelia Anne Towes kept a girls' boarding school at Lombard House; in mid-century a lodging-house was there; in 1897 its owner, John Harrington, granted a lease to the Hertford Conservative & Liberal Unionist Club. 1844 saw Dimsdale's house leased to the Literary & Scientific Institute, who had moved from Fore Street for their meetings and library. By 1850 their secretary was George Towers, a doctor at the Infirmary, and a Sunday painter. In 1866 the books were transferred to the temporary public library at the Corn Exchange and No.16 became the Armoury for the Volunteer Rifles until 1898 when the Drill Hall, Port Hill was built. In 1832 John Davies, a pioneer in plastic surgery was practising in Bull Plain. He gave his name to Davies Street.

The wooden Folly Bridge was replaced with brick in 1860; five years later it was planned to extend the Great Eastern Railway to Bull Plain. This was approved, but never carried out. No.20 was sold to Miss Thornton in 1884 and the Mission Room built. In 1898 the Waterside property was purchased by McMullens and the house, badly damaged, was pulled down in 1917. The riverside cottages remain.

Twentieth century changes: From 1903 Hertford Museum had been housed in the offices of R.T. & W.F. Andrews at No.56 Fore Street. In 1913 they bought No.18 Bull Plain, known as 'Walton House' from Thomas Pamphilon and the museum opened there in February 1914. The brothers acted as curators and when R.T. died in 1926, his son, H.C. Andrews, managed the museum helped by Mr. Robins, an

Bull Plain after the Zeppelin bomb of the 13th October 1915. 'Waterside' is left, the Hertford Conservative Club right. (Hertford Museum Collection HETFM: 6036.213).

enthusiastic antiquary and the owner of Dicker Mill.

On October 13th 1915, at night, a Zeppelin L16 dropped 14 high explosive and 30 incendiary bombs on Hertford. The third high explosive bomb fell outside the entrance gates of the Conservative Club. Walter Hoare, dental surgeon of St. Andrew Street:

I was at the Conservative Club last night ... with Mr. Starr Wood, Reggie Willson, Mr. Sinden, Mr. Gifkins, Mr. John Hammond and others. We stood outside watching a Zeppelin overhead. Then suddenly we heard a whizzing noise and the explosion of bombs dropping. We scattered in all directions. I got into the Club and stayed there for 10 minutes. When I came out everything was in darkness and I found some bodies lying in the lobby. I saw somebody strike a match and heard him say it was Mr. Jevons and also by a match I recognised Mr. Jolly. (*Hertfordshire Mercury*, January 18th, 1919).

Those killed were the Borough Surveyor Henry Jevons, 57, All Saints' Organist James Gregory, 55, draper George Cartledge, 56, Barclay's Bank cashier Ernest Jolly, 27, Mr. Spicer, a labourer standing in Bull Plain, and George Game, aged 4, killed in bed at No.37. Mr. Gifkins of North Crescent was badly injured, losing an eye and a hand. Mr. Searles sustained severe shock as well as injuries. All adjacent buildings were badly damaged, especially the Club and Waterside. Gravesons lost their windows and the Mission Hall clock stopped at 10 o'clock, the exact time of the impact. A portion of the club gatepost was hurled up on to a shop roof in Fore Street. Reg Cull, aged 96, speaking in 1992: "That's where we lost the cream of the town, that day."

Mrs. Doll Cunningham, née Thomason, recounted in 1994 a story told by her older sister Bessie. The family were living in Bull Plain in 1915.

> Uncle Will had come home on leave from the army and he slept under the window. When the bomb fell it threw him out of the window. Mum was in her night-dress and whether she tried to pick my uncle up or what, but she got the mark of a hand, in blood, on her night-dress. But we don't know any more than that. (Uncle Will, who was known as Riley Clark, survived the ordeal.) Bessie's rag doll was in the museum – they took it out of the house that was bombed ... but I doubt it's there now, it would be moth-eaten.

Thomas Pamphilon, plumber and fire captain, sold No.18 to the Andrews Brothers in 1913, as premises for a museum. He had purchased it from John Harrington in 1893 after moving across from No.25. Grandaughter Joan Pamphilon remembers:

> My father, Harry, lived at No.9 as a batchelor before he married my mother in 1915, the same week as the Zeppelin bomb fell. All the wedding presents were out and they were covered in glass. They were married on the same day that the burials of the people killed took place. My brother and sister and I were all born at No.9 and I left there when I was about six to live for a time in Railway Street. I can remember the Salvation Army playing in Bull Plain and we had a dog who, if we weren't careful, would go out and join them – he'd sit in the middle and howl! When the fair used to come, we'd sit in the sitting-room upstairs and the swings practically came up to the windows. And do you remember that man who used to make some sort of toffee? He'd throw it over a hook and pull it. And we didn't all die of it, did we? I'm sure he'd licked his hands before he pulled it.

Below: Harry Pamphilon's letter heading (Hertford Museum Collection).

Joan Pamphilon's father, Harry, moved the business to No.9 after the sale of No.18 by her grandfather, Thomas.

Mary Ollis' great-grandfather, John Rose, transferred his printing works to Rose's Corner (now Oddbins) from Fore Street near today's Midland Bank. Sidney, his son who married Emma Marks, took over the business. Mary recalled her mother's tale of shooting water pistols with her brother, out of the window, at Tory gents making for Hertford Club. In the 1930s, the Countess of Strathmore came to Hertford, bringing Princesses Elizabeth and Margaret with her. They both visited Rose's to buy postcards with their pennies. Joe Quince remembered:

"When I moved into Bull Plain there was us in No.21 and Mrs. Johnson in No.19. When a person died, someone would come and tap on the door and mother and Mrs. Johnson would go there and scrub them and put them in boxes for 2/6d a time. Mrs. Johnson'd got a backyard with a drain in the middle. She had a cold tap and a big old steel copper and she'd put wood under it and boil water and she would take and starch all these gents' shirts from the Salisbury – dickies – all polished starch. She would spend hours ... all flat-irons, mind. *Joe's stepfather was 'Whisper' Wright*—In the kitchen he'd got a small range: oven, fire, then a top. They would get a big old galvanised can and a pig's head and put it there Monday and by Friday all you could see was the teeth showing and they made their brawn. What is now the C.A.B., in there, that used to be the 'Band of Hope & Glory'. If you were drunk they took you in and said a little prayer. They'd give you a lead medal with a ribbon and say you were saved."

Whisper was the caretaker of the 1930s-built Arcade. He took a great pride in it, sweeping and discouraging cycling – as Ellen Quince said "If kids went down there on their bikes, he'd shove a broom through the wheel." Peter Ruffles remembered:

"There was always a warm welcome for the paper-boy at 19 Bull Plain in the '50s – whether it was as Dinksie Johnson was leaving at 7.20 to walk to work at Simsons in Parliament Square – or a Saturday morning much later to collect the money for the week's *Daily Mail* delivery. The form was to ride your bike on to the pavement, foot on step, knock the heavy knocker at the top of the door, then open the door to the passage/hall within. It was usually Mary, her legs swathed in bandages who'd come laughing from the kitchen at the back; sometimes old Mrs. Johnson. There was always a bright exchange and a hand-over of the correct cash.

I remember remarking how Miss Dinksie Johnson's hips both touched the side of the hallway as she approached, if it were she who answered the knock. She was always dressed in black and wore a black hat – which from the rear in the street, resembled an advert popular at the time for Sandeman's Port – a dark silhouette. Because of her dimensions, the walk up Bull Plain and Maidenhead Street was slow and rather grand. The other remarkable feature for the teenage paper boy's impression was her milk-white complexion. Sadly I was caught up in the alarm at her death. I knocked as usual, tried to open the door but couldn't. I went for the one and only time round to the back, by going down to the clinic and finding my way around. I told whoever it was in the kitchen of my problem. They then went to find Dinksie collapsed behind the door."

Don Geall tells how his family came to Bull Plain:

"One Sunday in 1929 Mum and Dad came on the train from Liverpool Street to Hertford East. They looked round the town, then Dad said 'I'd like a cup of tea, we'll try and find a café.' But they couldn't. 'This town needs a café', said my Dad, a trained pastry-cook and wedding-cake maker. They found two prospective sites, one in Bull Plain and one in Maidenhead Street. Dad wrote a letter and got the one in Bull Plain, No.11. (He called it George's). I was born there, along with my two brothers.

They started literally without anything: as Dad took the money for cups of tea, bacon sandwiches, or whatever, Mum ran round to Peark's in Maidenhead Street to purchase new supplies. That's how they got started. They used to open 7 days a week – Sunday 'til 2 o'clock – and get all the men, mostly men who lived by themselves, a dinner; Saturday nights until the dances were thrown out and used to serve egg and chips. They had some lady customers, not a lot. It was a café where they played crib

Don Geall sitting in the carrier of a Graveson's trade bike, circa 1935 with Harry 'Curly' Foster from Folly Island. The latter was killed in Java in 1943 and has no known grave. (Reproduced with the kind permission of Jill Geall.)

and cards. When the Assizes were on at the Shire Hall and the prisoners were in the cells, their food used to come from Dad's and he would prance along with his trays of dinners. Now, Cook's a very famous name in Hertford. They used to have a fruit stall in Bull Plain on Hinds side. When the Arcade opened, they had the big corner shop opposite my father's café. It was all specially constructed, with a lovely show of fruit. Then they went into Rose's on the corner." (Don's father gave up the café in 1939 suffering from exhaustion; his call-up was deferred until 1942. After the war he worked for Bob Cook.)

Frank Chappell bought Webb's Newsagents, No.5, in 1960 and remained until 1980. "Webbs started selling Sunday papers when it was a disgrace to take a Sunday paper (1930s); you were frowned on if you bought a paper. But trade gradually improved because when I took over, I had 28 boys! No wonder I'm thin on top!" Frank then introduced toys: "In 1960 you had to climb three steps to get into the shop, which was no good for a toy shop, they'd want to bring a pram in. So I had the floor sunk to walk level." Peter Ruffles remembered the shop:

"I remember buying some goggles from Webbs, which are still in the back of my Honda. They were kids' muck-about goggles and I wanted them for my push-bike in the snow. I suppose I wore them a dozen times in serious stuff but I still carry them around in case I'm on the motor bike and there's a sudden storm. I can picture them now, in Webb's window."

Well-remembered businesses of the earlier 20th Century were numerous. Tommy Ellis 'T. E. Ellis, Tobacconist & Fancy Goods' at No.6, where the family were hairdressing in 1886: Peter Ruffles says

"… he retained longer than any other shop in town the oil/converted to gas lamp above his shop in Bull Plain. Before the advent of municipal street lighting all the shops had to do the best they could to illuminate their entrances, and also, incidentally, their windows. Many kept them until the post-war years, while electric power cuts were a risk (Woolworth's interior lighting). Tommy Ellis' the last, was hit by a lorry in the early '60s. I got a picture in the nick of time."

James Seymour, taxidermist, was at No.12 (did he supply stuffed creatures to the museum?); Rose's, stationers at No.2 founded by Henry Rayment in 1888, and giving its name to Rose's Corner; Webb's newsagents at No.5, starting as greengrocers at No.11 by 1918; Edmund Roche, uncle to 'Eddie' followed by Reg Hayden, both shoe repairers at No.9; the White House Dairy at No.3 and later when Boots took over, at No.15. No.8 housed Mr. Rowley, who gave his name to Rowley's Road, near to where he kept horses; Creaseys, established by 1920; 'George's café, opened in 1929; Morris's crammed furniture depot at No.16; Bull Plain Clinic emerged in 1932, followed by the Arcade and at this time the Mission Room became All Saints' Mission Hall and also accommodated a branch of the Oddfellows.

During World War II Rose's let a room to the Red Cross, the British Legion and the Soldiers' Sailors' & Airmen's Families Assn. all supervised by Mrs. Blackett-Ord. From the *Hertfordshire Mercury*, January 17th 1941 – "Light from the Museum. For an unscreened light which shone from Hertford Museum during the black-out on December 14th, Herbert Andrews of 25 Castle Street was fined 10/-d at Hertford Borough Court yesterday."

Later businesses were Arcade Boot & Shoe (Roche & Hayden); Cooks, greengrocers; Mina Brown, hairdresser, Chappell's Toys at No.5; Canvas Holidays – today's new 'Stonehouse'; and the Enfield Highway Cooperative at No.16. This latter property was saved from demolition by designation as a listed building in 1953 resulting from intervention by Harold Macmillan. Eighteen years later it was purchased by Beadle Holding Properties and restored to more than its former glory by architects Thorne, Barton, Kirby & Nash and builders Henry Norris & Son. It was renamed Beadle House. No.2, Rose's, was restructured in 1983-4 but at the same time Nos.4-14 were demolished and new properties built as part of the Central Area Redevelopment.

Acknowledgements: Hertford Museum, HALS, *Hertfordshire Mercury*, *EHAS Transactions* and all the Hertford Oral History 'interviewees'.

Chapter 5
THE MUSEUM IN THE 1940s:
A CHILDHOOD RECOLLECTION
by Edgar Lake

The Museum was one of the joys of my childhood. I was born a few doors away at Lombard House. My earliest excursions with my father were to Warboys' sweet shop to buy chocolate drops. This short walk along Bull Plain took us past the Museum, and we would often call in to see Mr. Legget the Custodian. The porch was then occupied by the pilasters from the Old Coffee House Inn (demolished 1938). The musty smell of the oak would greet us as we reached the door, and I was slightly in awe of the one with the face. In later years I was puzzled as to why she had only one breast. My father loved to talk and view the latest acquisitions. The new gifts always went on display with the walls and cases becoming increasingly crowded. For me as a small child there was much to delight and amuse. Things would be lit up for me. There was a light in the dolls' house. There was also one in the model of the old All Saints' Church. My father could remember the night it burnt down. It was said that the model was completed only a few days before the fire (December 1891). I loved the musical box with the dancing monkey, the orrery, and the zoetrope. They all worked and I liked their names. The zoetrope produces a moving image when set spinning. The Museum owned a small working printing press and this provided printed souvenirs for visitors.

The display was quirky but instructive. One case had antiquities from Egypt including embalmed hands and feet. It also contained mummified animals found locally beneath floorboards and in chimneys, amongst them a cat. The case with the prehistoric flint implements included material on a local forger, with his picture, and examples of his arrow heads. I thought that they looked better than the genuine article. That was an early and useful lesson. The Museum had a corner devoted to old All Saints' Church apart from the model. Half a wall was covered with pictures of the church, and there was a case of items saved. I liked the wall of guns and weapons. There was a case of dolls and fine needlework. Interesting furniture formed part of the display. There was a gothic cabinet with strange items of china within. Scrap drives to aid the war effort were part of daily life. Railings were being removed from gardens and churchyards and taken to scrap yards. Luckily H.C. Andrews visited the Tewin dump, and was allowed to remove two firebacks and two cannon. When I look at them now I am amazed that they could easily have been destroyed. Their rescue was celebrated by the production of postcards. With hindsight this was an astute move as the removal of scrap was rarely permitted.

Front view of Hertford Museum, c.1948 (Hertford Museum Collection HETFM: 6037.352)

In 1940 Longmore School was bombed. I was then at Faudel-Phillips Infants and for a time 'school' became a private house. Attendance was only required in the morning. As a result of the bomb the bust of Ceres had to be removed from the Corn Exchange facade. She was installed in the Museum porch on top of a butterfly cabinet, and the pilasters moved into the museum. Sadly she was later moved into the garden where she suffered from the weather.

Also in 1940 my father acquired an allotment. This was in a walled garden behind the Museum. It was owned by H.C. Andrews who had dreamed of having an extension to the Museum on the site. It was divided into four plots. The other three were let to Mrs. Johnson. She was the matriach of a large family and she lived at 19 Bull Plain. She was not pleased to have my father on site and initially accused him of taking over too much land. The soil was superb and we 'dug for victory' producing asparagus and strawberries. Mrs. Johnson's daughter 'Dinks' did even better, growing flowers! For me the allotment produced an endless supply of items: shells, rocks, fossils and corals, that had been thrown out of the collection. These I carefully gathered up, washed and took into the Museum for indentification. This was great fun as I would be taken upstairs and shown a similar example to one of my objects in one of the cabinets. I loved the upstairs. It was filled with all kinds of stuffed birds and animals. These stood on storage cabinets full of everything from the natural world that it is possible to collect. I liked the fish in the bow fronted cases. They seemed preserved for ever against their background of weeds. Gilt lettering on the cases gave details of the fisherman, date and weight of fish. The pike was magnificent. To my sorrow a later curator removed them all from their cases. The allotment even had a resident fox when my father hired it. It was stuffed and it went under the compost heap. I expect my father feared that I would take it home. There was no easy access to the allotment, we reached it via the Arcade and Bircherley Green. There was no documentation with regard to our hire of the land. The rent was paid by cash and went straight into H.C. Andrews' pocket. This caused considerable anxiety to the next owners, the Borough Council. In 1949 they produced a full legal agreement for our use of the garden. It was an interesting site because although part of the most densely populated area of the town, it had never been built on.

The allotment brought us into contact with the already mentioned Johnson family. Mrs. Johnson had two daughters living at home. Dinks was a very large lady who worked at Simpson Shand. She and her mother lived in the front room and kept watch over Bull Plain. A 'simple' daughter Mary, did all the work and lived in the kitchen. It was a source of wonder that Mary never left the house. She would scrub the front step from inside the hallway. Wartime regulations demanded that she should have a job. It was fortunate that at this point the Museum cleaner, Mrs Taylor from No.17, retired. Mary was then persuaded to cross the street and take over the work.

On 2 July 1944 a flying bomb exploded at Mill Bridge. This smashed windows throughout the town, including those at the Museum. The response was to have small windows and these were filled with a row of very large meat dishes. Now expensive items, they were then of very little value. I loved them, studied them on my way home from school and soon started collecting them myself. Today I am sure, the windows would be left empty, but it was part of the spirit of the age to make things as normal as possible.

During the war years Hertford's most favoured tea rooms was Christine's Café in Fore Street. These had been Evan Marks, the jewellers, and they were lined with glass cases. As a 'shop window' for the Museum these were filled with objects from the collection. I remember that on being taken there as a child I was slightly shocked that anything should leave the hallowed walls on Bull Plain.

The war years saw the return of H.C. Andrews to Hertford. He was a wonderful man and he had a profound influence on me. Badly disabled by a stroke in 1942, he fought hard to recover and he was always in the Museum. When I was ten I decided that I wanted to write a history of Lombard House. My father arranged for me to see H.C. and I visited him regularly for the next two years by which time I had a history of the house carefully written out in a blue notebook. To my great delight William Le Hardy, the County Archivist included it in a display of local history. By this time I was collecting shells and butterflies. H.C. Andrews would often give me shells for my collection, and I would spend hours upstairs looking at the butterflies and moths.

As I grew older I would discover things in the collection that I had never noticed before. The Museum owns a group of painted panels from a house in Railway Street. These were dark and mysterious but it was still possible to make out that they showed classical figures in a landscape. They stood behind a row of display cases on the ground floor. I now know that they are a rare example of room decoration from about 1700. Then there was the attic. This was a room I rarely saw. It was chaotic. I remember in particular a large display case of dolls and fabrics from Japan. I assume that they had been given by Bishop Andrews. When I saw them they were falling apart as a result of the ravages of the clothes moths. Moths were a real problem then and all museums had a strong smell of moth balls.

The Museum lacked a defined collection policy. I remember the arrival of the ivory prayer mat, a gift from the MP, Rear Admiral Sir Murray Sueter. It was large, took up too much room, and displaced other exhibits. One gift I particularly liked was the fragment of cloth, part of the decoration in Westminster Abbey for the 1937 Coronation. For me the fact that it had 'been there' made it very special.

The holy of holies was the office. This was an area partitioned from the rest of the Museum and lined with books. H.C. Andrews sat at a central table that was piled high with books, papers and specimens. He had difficulty moving around, but he could find any book he wanted without recourse to an index. He loved Hertford and he loved the Museum. It was this enthusiasm that encouraged local people to donate their treasures. By the time H.C. Andrews died the building was packed solid from attic to cellar with the collection. Everything was carefully labelled and the arrival of new items was recorded. Bad times were to follow.

I remember looking from the allotment into the Museum garden one evening shortly after the collection had been passed into the hands of the Borough Council. To my horror I noticed a bulging dustbin. I was over the wall in a flash. I found that the bin was full to overflowing with booklets and magazines. Worse was to follow. Holes were dug in the garden and filled with shells and minerals. After this I was a frequent visitor to the Museum garden. Anything that caught my eye I retrieved, took home and treasured. I wish now that I had collected more. A few years ago I returned the polished mineral specimens. It was a wrench after having them for so many years but it gave me pleasure to return them to their true home. I can see now that the folk charged with the care of the collection had no idea how to cope with it. It should be remembered that there was no museum store. Any institution that has lasted a hundred years will have known both good and bad times. It gives me satisfaction to witness at firsthand the very high quality of care now being given to the collection. It bodes well for the future.

Chapter 6
THE SOCIAL HISTORY AND ETHNOGRAPHIC COLLECTIONS
by Helen Gurney

Hertford Museum cares for over 50,000 objects and only about 3-4% of these are normally on display. The remaining objects are housed in our Seed Warehouse store in six rooms. The entire Hertford Museum collection is made up of smaller collections relating to subject areas. The two collections which are of particular personal interest to me are one of the largest – Social History – and also one of the smallest and most diverse – the Ethnographic collection.

Toasters, toys and tools

Social History is concerned with how people have lived their lives and how and why their experiences and behaviour have changed over time. It is concerned with the nature of family life, work and consumer behaviour.

It would be possible to write a whole book or a series of books about the social history collections at Hertford Museum, because they are so diverse and vast. It is hoped that this will serve as a taster for those interested to know just what lurks in the darkness of the Museum's stores and ways in which the museum collects such fascinating snippets of people's past.

The social history collections have been growing since the museum was founded, when local people brought in objects such as kitchen equipment, decorative items that might have taken pride

Mangles in the Social History Collection in the Seed Warehouse Stores.

of place on someone's mantelpiece or an object relating to a job or profession, for instance toothbrushes that were produced in a local factory.

Within living memory

As a museum curator, there is nothing more gratifying than to see visitors pointing at objects with a warm sincerity and reminiscing about 'how my mother used to use one in our house exactly the same as that'. What is so important about social history collections is not just the objects themselves, but the personal story that they tell. When the museum takes objects in, we always ask the donors to give as much information as possible about the person who used it, wore it or owned it, and maybe ask them to bring in a photograph, or maybe get a person's reminiscence down on tape.

Compare these two labels. Which would you most likely to find more interesting?

Toy fire engine	**Toy fire engine (tin plate with box)**
Tin plate complete with box c1964	Bought as a Christmas present for Johnny Bloggs for 2d from Hertford shop on Hertford Street in 1964, by his mother Cynthia. Cynthia worked in Hertford Shop from 1959 to 1971, when it closed down. This is now Hertford Clothes shop.

Some of the collections are even more emotive and may bring back troubled memories. The museum has a growing collection of objects relating to the Second World War and the Home Front, for instance, photographs of bomb damage in Hertford, ration books, gas masks and blackout curtains. Not only do these objects tell us about the Home Front, but they can be used as learning tools for schools.

Please touch

The museum is in the process of putting together 'handling collections' so that schools and groups can get closer to objects by touching, smelling and feeling them. The Victorian handling collection has been particularly successful, and children get first hand experience of what life was like as a Victorian maid with objects relating to cleaning, washing and ironing. These objects can also be used in reminiscence sessions for the elderly. The process of reminiscing is not just the act of remembering, but also the act of communicating and sharing in the context of sensitive attention by others.

It can also be educational and enjoyable: creating a context for interaction between young and old. Other areas that the museum is building upon are WW2 and the Home Front, toys and the 1950s. Once these collections have been built up it is

Objects from the Victorian Handling Collection

hoped that the museum will embark upon reminiscence projects with the local community.

The Addis Collection of Toothbrushes

The Addis factory on Ware Road was one of the most important industries in Hertford from 1919 right up until 1996. Addis was the oldest firm of brushmakers in the world. The Museum had previously been given photographs relating to the factory and the workers and in 2002 they were given over 3,000 toothbrushes that came from the Addis Factory stores. The toothbrushes represent over 150 years of technological achievement in toothbrush design and productivity, ranging from the early bone toothbrushes that were filled by hand to modern plastic versions.

Museum volunteers have catalogued each toothbrush precisely with the expert help of Robin Addis and eventually some will go on display. This collection, together with photographs and archives, provides a very real history of the Addis business and the workforce of Hertford. To complement this collection, the Hertford Oral History Group and the Museum are working together to tape the memories of the ex-workers from the Addis Factory.

Collecting for the future

As a museum, we do not just collect items from the distant past. We aim to collect items from recent decades too, so that in 100 years time, people may be able to see on display an exhibition of everyday objects from a 2000 home, such as a DVD player, electric toothbrush, clothes and photographs. As well as this is the need to show contemporary society in Hertford and the surrounding areas, for example, events, clubs, professions and fashion.

Ethnography

As soon as Hertford Museum was established, many people donated all manner of things to the museum. Ethnography is concerned with the study of human societies. Hertford Museum's ethnographic collection reflects the collecting and missionary activities of the late 19th and early 20th Century residents of East Herts. Members of the Andrews family were connected with work abroad, as Walter Andrews (another Andrews Brother) was Bishop of Hokkaido and John Batchelor was a missionary, both of whom donated items to the Museum on their return. Many well-to-do families travelled abroad and brought back 'souvenirs' from their colonial travels. The Museum now holds a collection of objects from as far afield as central Africa, Japan and New Zealand.

Most of these items were collected in the 19th and early 20th Centuries, and include arms and armour, costume, jewellery, musical instruments and religious artefacts. We no longer actively collect this type of material, but it is an important part of the museum's collecting history.

There are approximately 1,000 ethnography objects that were collected during 1901-1935. Mostly hand-made, these represent many different diverse cultures and traditions, some of which have long since disappeared. Two outstanding items include a late 19th Century Royal Siamese prayer mat of plaited ivory strips measuring just under 2 metres long and a suit of Samurai Armour.

This collection is far from being properly interpreted and needs detailed research in order to understand fully the breadth of this fascinating collection. It is important as representative of past collecting fashions of the Museum's history, to understand everyday and ceremonial life of different cultures and to appreciate the technical and aesthetic accomplishments of these societies.

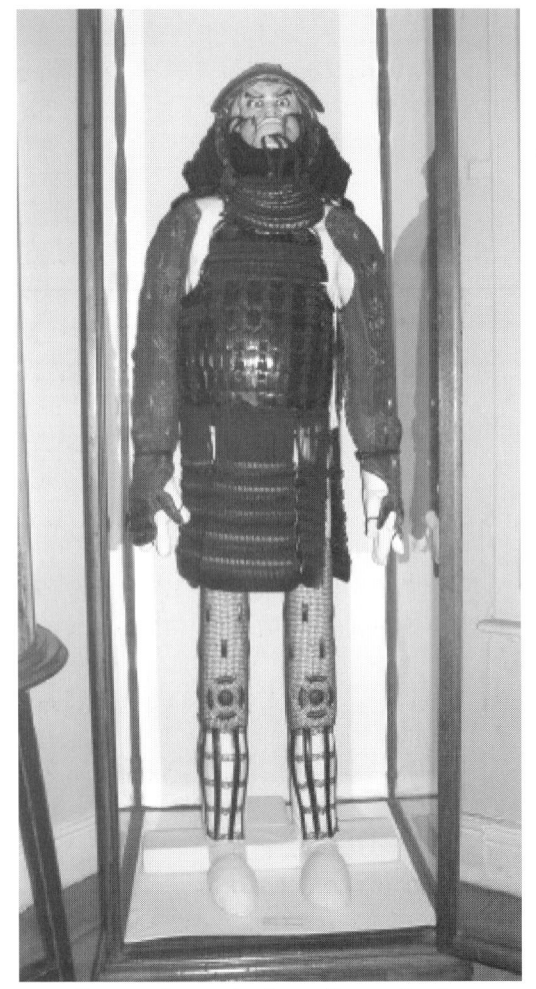

Samurai warrior's outfit on display (HETFM: 5625.1)

Chapter 7

THE POSTCARD AND PHOTOGRAPH COLLECTION
by Margaret Harris

Hertford Museum is fortunate in having a large collection of postcards and photographs, dating from the mid 19th Century to the present day, and this collection forms a very important part of the archive of the museum. As well as the aesthetic quality of many of these images, they make a valuable record of our surrounding area by allowing us to glimpse into the past and observe the changing way of life and customs of local people. The collection also charts the history of the different processes of photography.

Postcards

Some years ago, before the modern offices replaced an earlier extension at the back of the museum, there existed a tiny quaint attic known to the staff as the back attic. In this attic was a tall chest of drawers where many of the picture postcards were stored. These had been carefully mounted on cartridge paper in fours, probably by W.F. Andrews, one of the museum founders. Other postcards were contained in a bound album. With today's knowledge of conservation, they have been removed and are now stored using approved materials, in alphabetical order so as to make access easier for the public, their details recently entered on the museum computer. This work was largely done with the help of volunteers.

There are now about 5,000 postcards, most of them collected by W.F. Andrews between 1902 and 1905, the height of postcard production. Many of those that he collected were samples from postcard companies, and others were from members of his own family and from friends. They cover most towns and villages in Hertfordshire, and usually picture the most important buildings in that location. For example, many scenes show the church, the public house, the High Street, the local country house and, later, the cinema.

This collection has so far proved very popular with museum visitors who are often able to choose a picture of their street, village or town, and have a copy made. Although most of the early postcards are sepia or black and white, some were hand coloured. The staff has continued to collect up until the present day, both old and modern examples.

Photographs

There are now well over 6,000 photographs in the Hertford Museum collections, and these mainly, but not always, have a local connection. One of the earliest photographic images in the museum is a stereoscopic Daguerreotype, dating between 1840 and 1860, which portrays a girl wearing a green dress and white veil. This process was introduced in 1839 by L.J.M. Daguerre, and produced a very fragile surface on a metal support that could be easily scratched, so was usually enclosed in a metal case. Unfortunately the provenance of the example in the Museum collection is unknown. Another very early group of photographic prints shows scenes of Hertford Castle and Hertingfordbury, and these were printed from a collection of waxed paper negatives, which date from 1857. The photographer was William Robert Baker of Bayfordbury, one of the pioneers of photography and owner of a Fox Talbot camera, named after the inventor of another early process, the calotype. There are also representations in the collections of many other early photographic methods, including ambrotypes, albumen prints, platinum prints and collodion processes, and identifying these processes can help in dating the photographs.

Much of the original photographic collection was stored in albums entitled 'Old Faces' and 'Old Places'. We have a lot to thank the founders of the museum for in that they usually dated these images, therefore making documentation easier. Although in recent years the photographs have been removed from the albums, the page numbers were retained so that the old index could still be used, and the original albums have been kept. Once again, a group of volunteers made a valuable contribution to this task. The photographs themselves have been mounted and stored using acid free card and boxes, and all the details are now entered on to the computer to allow for easy searching.

'Old Faces', as the name suggests, is a comprehensive collection of images of notable locals including tradesmen, doctors, nurses, clergymen, military, gentry and many others. They mostly date from the late 19th century, and a large number were in the form known as a *Carte de Visite*, introduced in England in 1858. These were photographs mounted on card, usually with the photographer's name included and were originally intended as visiting cards, as well as a way of advertising the photographer. However, these *Carte de Visite* soon became desirable objects, and collecting them quickly became a craze, known as cartomania. A larger version, the cabinet card, of which the museum also has many examples, was introduced in 1866 but was never quite as popular.

There were two volumes of 'Old Places', which contained a record of buildings and some of the important events of the past, mostly in and around Hertford. The first volume contained images dating for the most part from the 1880s, although there are a few earlier photographs in this album. Volume II went up to the late 1940s, the theme being the same as Volume I and also includes many scenes taken

Remains of old All Saints Church re-erected after the fire, in the garden of Elsden, Queens Road, Hertford (Hertford Museum Collection HETFM:6182.134)

from the new council housing estates springing up around Hertford. Some, in the earlier album especially, record buildings before they were demolished, many taken by the Elsden family firm, which illustrates the foresight of the early curators and photographers in keeping a record for posterity of the town as they knew it. This practice has continued up to the present day, including collections of photographic surveys of the town before the Gascoyne Way was constructed in 1964. One such collection was photographed by Gordon Davies, a former curator at the museum, and similarly, another produced by a member of the Hertford and District Camera Club on the same theme. Later, the highway engineering consultant firm, Mouchel, gave the museum their own photographic survey of Hertford before major sewage replacement work was carried out in the early 1970s. These town surveys are invaluable to the staff at the museum, and are used frequently when answering the numerous local history enquiries that are received each week. The present staff also keeps up to date with changes in the area by photographing buildings due for demolition, or sites that are to be built over.

There are other photographic surveys deposited in the museum, including many aerial photographs of Hertfordshire from the 1960s and 1970s. Some of these were carried out for the purpose of identifying archaeological sites. Other surveys include the negatives for the Listed Building Survey of 1989, produced by East Herts District Council.

As well as albums and collections, the museum has many loose photographs. These are divided broadly into three main categories, topographical, portraits and events, and military. As with the albums the topographical group records many buildings from as far back as 1860. Some of these buildings do not exist now, but many still do, some surprisingly little changed. As well as Hertford, other towns and villages in the surrounding area are also represented. The early photographs particularly are of very high quality, especially those that used the platinum process, and in some cases these early photographs have survived better than later ones.

F.W. Taylor, the Muffin Man, Port Hill, Hertford, photograph by Sneesby, Fore Street, Hertford, from 'Old Faces' Album (Hertford Museum Collection HETFM: 6035.585)

The portraits and events collection not only shows notables of the town, but many special occasions that the ordinary town's folk have attended. These include royal celebrations such as Jubilee and Coronation dinners from Victoria to Elizabeth II, fairs, pageants, sporting events, processions and civic occasions. There are also photographs of workers at various local firms, for example McMullen's Brewery, Webb's Leather dressers and Addis Brushworks. There are family group pictures, dramatic societies, beating the bounds, Sunday School treats, fancy dress football matches and charabanc outings. Some of the most striking images of the more ordinary people include a tramp with his old pram which he used to push his possessions around, a road mender, Mr. Mardell, sitting in his wheelbarrow, and William Fell, known as Billy Chicken, delivering the *Hertfordshire Mercury* on his tricycle. Although many of these are of Hertford people there is a number from the surrounding towns and villages, and you could find amongst these an image of a village hedge layer, church bell ringer, clock winder, corn dolly maker, a ploughing match or a group of land girls.

Coronation Dinner, Drill Hall, Port Hill, Hertford, 1911, photograph by Elsden (Hertford Museum Collection : HETFM:6370.1.85)

The military photographic group dates from the nineteenth century, and a large proportion of the photographs was passed on to the museum together with many other military artefacts from the Hertfordshire Regiment in the 1960s. In this number are included formal pictures of high-ranking officers as well as regimental groups and informal scenes of the ordinary Tommy at army camp. There are also many portraits of those soldiers from the Hertfordshire Regiment honoured for bravery in the Great War including the two Victoria Cross winners, Corporal A. Burt, and Second Lieutenant F. E. Young. One interesting part of this collection is a box containing many lantern-slides made from plates that have survived from the Boer War. Over the years the museum has accepted many regimental photographs from private donors too, including several from the family of Acting Sergeant Alfred Branch, who won the Distinguished Conduct Medal in World War II. The Home Guard is also remembered in this group, although these are all formal group portraits. The latest acquisitions in the military group include two generous gifts donated in the year 2000. The first, passed on to the museum via the T. A. Centre in Hertford, includes more than two hundred photographs and letters of soldiers who served with the Hertfordshire Regiment in the Great War. The other gift from the Trustees of the

Bedfordshire and Hertfordshire Regiment T.A. and Militia Trust includes many photographs as well as regimental silver and other items.

In addition to the previously mentioned groups, Hertford Museum also owns other albums and collections donated by families and individuals. These include albums that detail the early travels of local people around Britain and abroad, which gives an interesting insight into the leisure pursuits of the middle classes in the late nineteenth and early twentieth centuries. There are collections from the Wigginton family, the Balfour family, Cyril Heath's photographs used in his numerous local books, Norman Hare, a *Hertfordshire Mercury* photographer during the 1930s, and a collection from the family of W. E. Johns who wrote the Biggles books. There are albums of photographs of Christ's Hospital School, which moved to Horsham in 1983, Tesco having since been built on the site. There are also eighty-eight official photographs of the Mayors of Hertford deposited in the museum in 1981, on loan from the Hertford Town Council.

The museum photographic collection cannot be discussed without a mention of those photographic pioneers that produced them. There were many excellent photographers in Hertford in the late nineteenth and early twentieth centuries including the Sneebys, Allen Foster, and Henry Newton, but probably the most well known were the Elsdens, father and son. In 1857, a Mr. J. Craddock set up his Photographic Institution in North Crescent, where Water's Garage now has its premises. This is believed to be the first professional photographic studio in Hertfordshire. In 1859 the business was taken over by Arthur Elsden from London, who advertised his services as "Photographist and Stereographist". He was also a French polisher, cabinet maker and maker of photographic equipment. When commissioned to work at Hatfield House he had to take with him a portable darkroom as those were the days of the wet plate, and he needed to prepare and process the plates on the premises. His

A newspaper cutting showing Elsden's Photographic Studio in Mill Bridge (Hertford Museum Collection)

equipment was packed on a trolley, which he would push there and back to Hatfield each working day. His son, Arthur Vincent later joined him in his business and took over in 1882, the studio having then moved to Mill Bridge. His most valuable contribution to the town was the recording of the changes in Hertford, started by his father. Hertford Museum is lucky to have a large collection of these photographs and lantern slides, work which was largely done at the Elsdens' own expense. Arthur Vincent also photographed many famous people and buildings throughout the county. Interestingly he was frequently employed by the Great Eastern Railway to take the beauty spots of East Anglia for their carriages. His legacy still carries on, for apart from the vast collection that the museum owns, slides of his work are still frequently shown at various clubs and societies in the town, and are frequently used for illustrating local books.

Arthur V. Elsden, Photographer (Hertford Museum Collection HETFM: 6035.279)

Arthur Vincent Elsden died in 1929, and much of his collection of plates and prints was eventually passed on to George Blake, another well-known Hertford photographer. Many local people will remember him for his excellent wedding and school portraits, especially in the 1950s and 60s, although he was by all accounts a highly successful commercial photographer too. Hertford Museum is indeed fortunate in owning many of his photographs and negatives, mainly studies of Hertford including the castle, the open-air swimming pool in Hartham, schools, local churches and other buildings, street scenes and many more.

A little known group of photographs and glass plates that the museum owns is a natural history collection, mainly very fine bird studies, taken by W. Bickerton, FRZS. He was the recorder of birds for the Hertfordshire Natural History Society and Field Club in the early twentieth century. He frequently gave lantern lectures on natural history and the museum also has a great many of his lecture notes and other related items. Many of these were given in 1914 by William Graveson, and others some years later in 1973 by Bickerton's daughter.

One valuable photographic record in the museum collections is contained in a leather bound album which was produced by members of the Hertford and District Camera Club and presented to the Hertford Borough Council in 1951 to commemorate the Festival of Britain. This album, entitled "Hertford Then and Now", was

Hertfordshire Bird Studies, Reed Warbler feeding young Cuckoo, by W. Bickerton FRZS (Hertford Museum Collection HETFM: 6186.3)

subsequently donated to the museum and contains thirty-two views of Hertford around 1900, and the same scenes pictured in 1950. The earlier images were taken from lantern-slides made by Arthur Vincent Elsden. To celebrate the Millennium it was decided to continue this tradition and make up another album with photographs of the same views in the year 2000, and leave space for an update in 2050. The photographs were again produced by members of the Camera Club, and the work of mounting them in the new album was undertaken by volunteers.

The museum has other links with the Hertford and District Camera Club and stores their entries for the Elsden Trophy, an award that is presented in alternate years by the Camera Club to its members. This trophy is presented to the winner of the competition for capturing the changes of life in Hertford during the previous year. The award was set up in 1983 by a member of the camera club, another well known Hertford photographer, whose work is represented in the museum collections, the late Len Green, who taught at the Cowper School, and later Simon Balle.

One very large section of the museum photographic collection is the vast number of glass plates, negatives and lantern-slides. Lantern-slide shows and lectures were a popular entertainment before the advent of cinema and television, and the invention of modern slide projectors. It is estimated that there are well over 3,000 glass plates and slides many of which were from the Elsden studio, as they can be identified by the corresponding print with Elsden's stamp that the museum owns. A great many of these slide and glass plates are stored in old purpose built chests of drawers, others in the original wooden or cardboard boxes. Research is being undertaken to catalogue this collection as much of it has not yet been identified. However, there are many entries in the old day-books that will assist in this task, and this promises to be a rewarding and exciting project, as many of these images have rarely been seen. One other way of tracking down the provenance of these collections is to study the numerous newspaper cuttings and journals in the museum library. For example, there is an entry in The East Herts Archaeological Society Transactions describing the 1,160 lantern slides of Hertfordshire buildings that were made to order by W. B. Gerish, a founder member of the Society. These were given to Hertford Museum in 1935. The vast number of others depict local places, people and events including flower shows, pageants, studies of local churches and many more.

Another early pastime which later caused another craze in the mid to late nineteenth century was the viewing of stereoscopic cards, and most middle class Victorian households would probably have had a collection of these together with a special viewer. These cards were produced in their thousands so it is hardly surprising that the museum has a large collection, together with a very fine elm wood viewer. Each of these cards consist of two images mounted side by side of the same scene taken from a very slightly different viewpoint, and when seen through a special viewer, a three dimensional effect is produced. Some of these views are local places, others show more exotic scenes or the celebrities of the day, including royalty.

As well as the special stereoscopic viewer, there are many other items connected with the subject of photography in the collection. There are cameras, one of the earliest dating from 1894, a magic lantern, rejoicing in the name of Phantasmagoria, and a Kinematograph, an early film projector. Old cine cameras and film are represented as well as modern video tapes. The museum also owns a rare example of a type of camera obscura, called a Royal Accurate Delineator, which was patented in 1788 by William Storer.

Staff have over the years built up a record of events and activities that have taken place in the museum by taking their own photographs. These images include private views of exhibitions, children's events, staff celebrations, changes in the display and garden areas, and major repair works to the building. The museum is also building up a photographic record of all the objects in the museum, using a very generous recent donation of a digital camera. As well as an important addition to the documentation files, it is hoped that these eventually will be made accessible to visitors and researchers, and will complement the educational handling collection that the staff is compiling.

The museum is continuing to add to the photographic collections and is always happy to accept not only early examples, but those produced more recently, although the policy is now to accept only those with a local connection. It must be remembered that when the first curators, Robert Thornton and William Frampton Andrews started this collection, photography was in its infancy, but they had the foresight to build it up for future generations, as the present staff aim to do.

Chapter 8
'PAPER' COLLECTIONS
by Rosemary Bennett

These contain a multitude of items that are classified under headings such as drawings, prints, and maps, etc. W.F. Andrews collected the majority although R.T. also contributed, and over the years these collections have grown with donations from the general public and selective purchasing by curators. No item, however important or trifling, would have been possible without the invention of paper. Hertford can be justifiably proud that the first paper to be made in this country was by John Tate, at Sele Mill in 1488. Five hundred years later, the International Society of Paper Historians held a conference at Balls Park to commemorate this truly historic event. It is fitting that there are, in the museum's collections, two pages printed on Tate paper. The text comes from the Chronicles written by Jean Froissart (1337–1410) in which he details the history of Western Europe from 1304 to 1400.

Paintings and Drawings

These include a large collection of unframed small topographical items brought together by W.F. Andrews. They primarily depict scenes in and around Hertford with lesser emphasis on more distant parts of Hertfordshire. It is the subject matter, and not the artist, that is important. This basic collection has been added to over the decades and now includes work by artists of national importance. In 1940 the National Art Collection Fund donated the watercolour painting by Thomas Rowlandson (1756–1827) of 'Hertford Market'. Rowlandson had obviously spent some time sketching in Hertford for a further two of his works were purchased in the 1980s. These are 'The Bell Inn' (now The Salisbury) which was acquired in 1984 and a scene showing the central courtyard of 'The Bull Inn' acquired in 1988. The Bull Inn stood on the corner of Maidenhead Street and Bull Plain. The watercolour painting of 'All Saints' Church, Hertford' by Thomas Underwood (1772–1836) was donated via the National Art Collections Fund in 1939. A surprise item is a particularly good portrait of Charles Dickens, by his daughter Kate Perugini (1838–1929), whose second husband was the Neopolitan artist, Charles Edward Perugini.

The artists, William and Richard Westall, were born in Hertford and to acknowledge this connection the museum, in the mid 1960s, purchased 'Margaret of Anjou' painted in 1801 by Richard Westall, R.A. (1765–1836). There is a commemorative blue plaque on the Westall's old home in West Street.

Particularly delightful are thirty watercolour sketches by George Towers (1802–1882). It is very probable that Dr. Towers started painting when he was appointed

Thomas Rowlandson, 'The Bell Inn at Hertford', watercolour, early 19th century (Hertford Museum Collection HETFM: 2131.1)

Resident Medical Superintendent of the Hertford County Hospital, when it first opened in 1834. Living on site, Towers would have been more-or-less permanently on call so it is not surprising that a number of his works depict views from the hospital and vistas to be seen from the nearby woods. His earliest work is primitive and somewhat garish but his true talent unfolds over the decades and he certainly had an eye for detail. Edward Archibald Brown, A.R.W.S. (1866 – 1935) is also represented in the collections. Brown was the Headmaster of the Hertford School of Art, which occupied the first floor of the present Hertford Library, from the 1880s until it closed in 1924. There is a large canvas showing the meads and a series of small studies in oil and some pencil sketches. Brown was a far superior artist than these few items suggest. Hertford Museum arranged a major exhibition of his work and appealed to the general public for loans. This brought to light some superb paintings from as far away at Dorset. E.A. Brown regularly exhibited at the Royal Academy and was known to have been friends with prominent artists such as Sir David Muir and Sir Alfred East. Paintings of local scenes by contemporary artists such as Trevor Chamberlain and Cyril Nicholson have been acquired in the past but sadly current prices now put these beyond the Museum's resources.

Hertford Museum also has a number of interesting sketchbooks by the Rev. Robert Hassell Newell (1778–1852) who had been a student of the Bedfordshire artist,

William Payne. Newell, who was the Rector of both Little Hormead and Great Hormead, illustrated his own publications with beautiful miniatures worked in sepia wash. Examples of his work, such as 'Letters on the Scenery of North Wales' published in 1821, are in the British Museum. His son Charles, who was his father's curate, had a special interest in church fonts, and there is a large collection of his studies in the Museum. Henry, Newell's other son, accompanied his father and brother on sketching holidays but it is very evident he had not inherited the family talent. Also living at Great Hormead at the same time as the Newell family, was James Wilcox (1778–1865), a retired London linen draper. Wilcox was a very able artist who is reputed to have had lessons from the watercolourist, Samuel Prout. His sketchbooks include scenes executed in pen and ink as well as those in watercolour. During his business life, Wilcox travelled a great deal, always taking a sketchbook with him and, after retirement, he and his children went on many sketching tours together. Some consider Wilcox designed the earliest form of cycle, which was made for his own use. It was a large machine and local lads were paid to push him uphill.

Last but by no means least, there is a collection of humorous ink sketches and other work by Starr Wood (1870–1944). Wood worked in advertising and for magazines such as *Punch* and also published magazines that he both wrote and illustrated. Wood liked to draw from life and would drag unsuspecting people from the street into his studio. Recognisable Hertford scenes and people are to be found in his work. Starr Wood lived in West Street and other West Street residents, with work in the collections, are Arthur Nicholls, a commercial artist whose family owned the brewery in West Street, and Annette Benson who is reputed to have been the first woman doctor to work in India.

Prints

The prints comprise an assortment of etchings, engravings, mezzotints, etc. Pride of place goes to a complete series of engravings of country houses and a view of 'The North Prospect of Hertford' by Jan Drapentier in 1699, for Henry Chauncy's *History of Hertfordshire*, published in 1700. Other topographical prints are catalogued and stored according to location and naturally the largest group are those relating to Hertford. The collection of portrait prints includes many Hertfordshire worthies and there is also a small collection of portraits of the Kings and Queens of England.

Maps

The W.F. Andrews collection of Hertfordshire maps is exceptionally good with very few omissions from the earliest printed, by the famous cartographer Christopher Saxton in 1577, through to Ordnance Surveys of the late 19th century. John Speed's map of 1610 has a small map of Hertford inserted in a top corner, that shows both the market crosses and the 'cage' (lockup). It indicates what Hertford was like all those years ago. The Andrew Drury and John Andrews famous map of Hertfordshire is

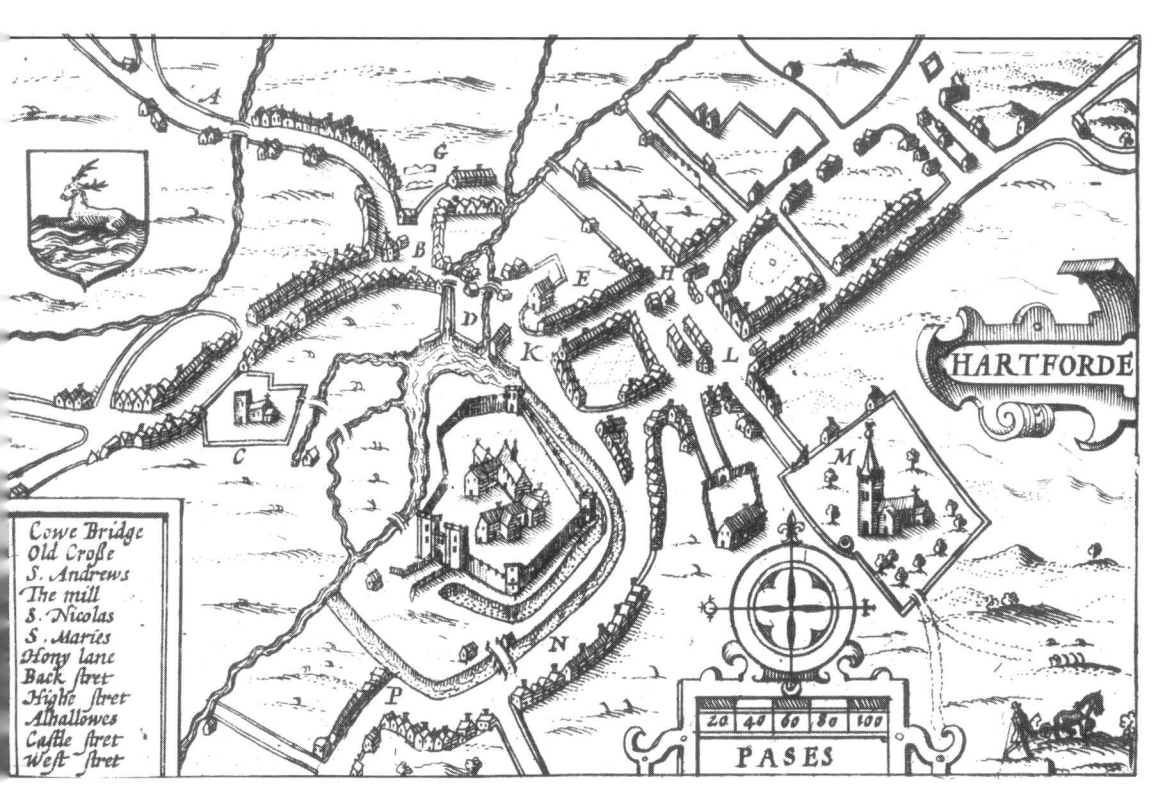

Copy of John Speed's Map of Hertford, 1610
(Hertford Museum Collection HETFM:6379.1)

made up of nine sections and was published in 1766. It has a lengthy title: 'A TOPOGRAPHICAL MAP OF HARTFORD-SHIRE, FROM AN ACTUAL SURVEY; In which is Expresse'd all the ROADS, LANES, CHURCHES, NOBLEMEN and GENTELMEN'S SEATS and everything remarkable in the COUNTY: TOGETHER, with the DIVISION of the PARISHES'. In addition there is a smaller collection of maps that belonged to R.T. Andrews.

Sermons

The collection of sermons and funeral orations, dating from the end of the 17th century through to the mid 19th century is, apart for one exception, connected with Hertford and Hertfordshire. Naturally they make sombre reading but the one exception is hilarious and was presumably kept for that reason. It was written by a very unimaginative Rev. Moore of Barton, Norfolk, for the funeral of Rev. Proctor, the former incumbent of the nearby Parish of Gissing. Moore obviously found the task extremely difficult. He relates that Mr Proctor had been a very poor young man when he arrived in the district and that he came "upon the back of a Dun Cow, it was not a Black Cow, nor a Brindled Cow, nor a Brown Cow. No beloved it was a Dun

Cow". Of Mrs. Proctor he writes that she was very good at making toast and "to spare the candle she would stir up the coals with her knitting pins"!

General Ephemera

The large collection of ephemera, particularly the 'small printings', is fascinating in more ways than one. Stephen Austin, grandson of the founder of the *Hertfordshire Mercury*, gave the core of the collection to W.F. Andrews way back in the 1870s. Today the company that still bears his name continues to lead the world with its ability to work in any alphabet and a multitude of languages, from Amharic to Zend. These small printings shed light on the every day life and customs of the late 18th century through to the mid 19th century. Spelling was not so precise in those days and was often phonetic. Hence there is a handbill calling all members of the Hartfordshire Militia to collect their trowsers. A timetable for the 'Regulator' stagecoach from Hertford to London recalls the days when the roads to London were crammed with stagecoaches with the wealthier sitting inside and the poorer sitting on the outside, exposed to the elements. As Stephen Austin kept a sample of all the print runs on a bill spike, there is a hole in the middle of each that adds to their charm. Many have the print run written and are signed by Austin, on the back. Some examples were lent to the British Museum for a small exhibition and a complete list is kept in the archive there. The exhibition was held when Stephen Austin and Co., now located on Caxton Hill, changed to using computers instead of the traditional hot metal press. The typefaces were donated to various museums and Hertford Museum received the Javanese.

Playbills dating from around 1800 advertise performances by strollers (travelling

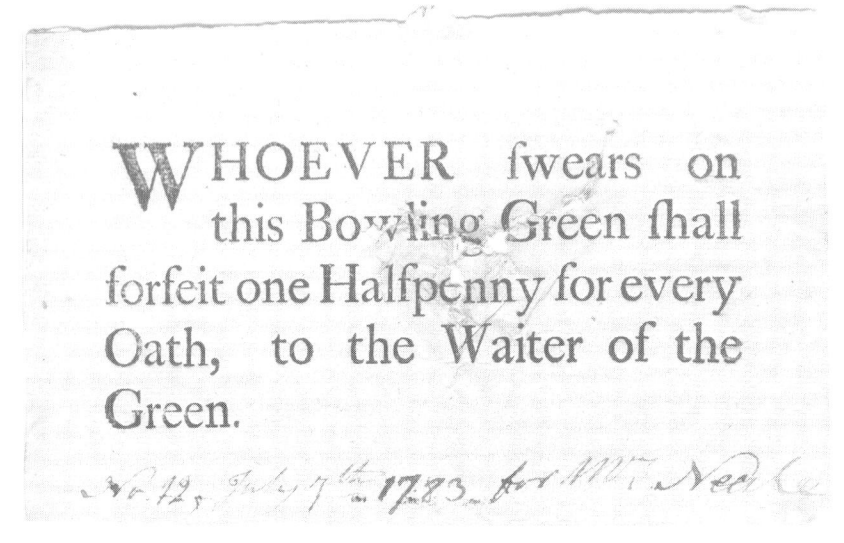

Notice of fine for swearing on the bowling green, 1783
(Hertford Museum Collection HETFM: 6245.99)

actors) at local inns. Later on in the 19th century, Hertford had its own amateur dramatic groups such as the 'Private Amateur Theatricals' and on a lower social level the members of The Literary Institute. Not surprisingly there were strict social divisions among Hertford's residents. The private theatricals programmes clearly state the time when carriages should be waiting at the door. The venue was usually the Shire Hall with tickets costing two shillings. During the same period the Literary Institute had its own amateur theatrical group. These usually took place in the Corn Exchange and tickets were often as little as sixpence. The very early 20th century seems to have been dominated by the fund raising supporters of the Hertfordshire Regiment until the onset of World War I. Perhaps this is the true origin of the Hertford Dramatic and Operatic Society, founded in 1919 and still flourishing.

Other items reflect the self-help society that existed before the welfare state. Those with a little money to spare would belong to one of the mutual benefit societies which met weekly at various inns in the town to enable members to pay their weekly subscriptions. Dr. Woodward organised his own Medical Club and another self-help society was The Coal Club. Many Hertford people would have lost their savings, with the collapse of the Hertford Bank in the 1850s. All the papers connected with the bankruptcy are owned by the museum but, like many other original documents, these are lodged with the county record office. This complies with guidelines issued by the Museums and Galleries Commission. In addition to being more easily available for research, these items also benefit from the specialist conservation and storage care that HALS (Hertfordshire Archives and Local Studies) provides. Other museum items, on deposit with HALS, include 17th century papers for placing Hertford's destitute children in apprenticeships. One would like to think these unfortunates had an easier time than Oliver Twist.

Election Posters

The Gilbertson Collection and the Hancock Collection, together with a mass of other posters from various sources, throw light on a rather shameful period of Hertford's past. Although there is later material, the mass is related to Hertford's parliamentary elections held in 1826, 1830, 1831 and 1832. Dr. Frances Page suggests, in the *History of Hertford* published in 1959, that this period was "perhaps the most controversial and corrupt in the whole of Hertford's history". The 1832 election was declared void and the Committee of Parliamentary Privileges refused to grant writs for a by-election. This resulted in Hertford, which until then had returned two members to Parliament, having no representation at all for the ensuing three years.

SHOCKING MISTAKE!

We think it our Duty to correct a Mistake which has appeared before the Public, respecting

A Dun Cow,

The Property of Messrs. INDEPENDENTO, *stating her to have been gored:*

IT IS TRUE, THAT A BULL

was turned into a Pasture belonging to the above Gentlemen— it was not known at that Time, that

The BULL was occasionally MAD!

as unfortunately it has proved,—During one of those paroxysms it came into his Noddle to make a furious attack upon the DUN COW, which she perceiving, dextrously avoided. The consequence was, the BULL'S HEAD came in contact with A CORPORATION POST, which not only fractured his HORNS, but inflicted a severe

WOUND IN HIS POLL:

The LAMBS, viewing the fearful Attempt of the *Mad Bull*, RAN AWAY.

N. B. DOCTOR ODD'S *Opinion respecting the* BULL, *we are happy to state*, *is, if the Wound does not Gangrene, it will merely produce a*

CONFIRMED POLL-EVIL.

[Austin and Sons, Printers, Hertford.]

Satirical election poster 'Shocking Mistake', 1826, printed by Stephen Austin (Hertford Museum Collection: HETFM: 4434.66)

Chapter 9

THE HERTFORDSHIRE REGIMENT AND OTHER MILITARY ITEMS
by Rosemary Bennett

The only regular regiment to be associated with Hertfordshire was the 49th Regiment of Foot. Raised in 1743 it was designated the 49th (Hertfordshire) Regiment of Foot for recruitment purposes, as the Colonel at the time came from Hertfordshire. The Regiment served in the Crimean War and a medal relating to this period, purchased in the 1960s, is in the Museum's collection. In 1881 the 49th was absorbed into the Berkshire Regiment.

The formation of the modern army started with an Act of Parliament in 1757 and the volunteer territorial force goes back to 1794. From early times it was the responsibility of the Lord Lieutenant of each county to call for volunteers when the country was under threat. Each troop would be under the command of a local landowner who was expected to pick up many of the costs. In the Museum collections there are some early 19th century items of exceptional quality belonging to the Standon Militia, such as a gorget, cloak clasp and dispatch case. They were collected by the Vicar of Standon, the Revd. Perowne, who had planned to start a small museum in the village. However this never happened and when he later moved to All Saints' Church, Hertford, these very interesting objects were donated to Hertford Museum.

In 1852, the Militia was reformed when the Lord Lieutenant of Hertfordshire, the Marquess of Salisbury, issued a request for volunteers. This was presumably due to the rumblings of discontent in Europe that led to the Crimean War. After a short period in Hatfield, the Hartfordshire Militia (phonetic spelling of Hertfordshire was always used) moved to Hertford into purpose built barracks in the London Road. In 1881 it was decreed that all volunteer battalions were to be annexed to the regular regiment that recruited in its area. Thus the Hartfordshire Militia was designated the 4th Battalion Bedfordshire Regiment (Hartfordshire Militia). The Museum has a number of items relating to this period, such as drums, and silver items that would have been used for grand occasions in the Officers' Mess. Sadly the memorial in All Saints' Church, Hertford, dedicated to those who gave their lives in the Crimean War was lost when the church was totally destroyed by fire in 1891. Fortunately the Museum has an old photograph of the memorial which researchers have found extremely useful. The Hertford Barracks continued to be used for various army purposes until after the 1939–1945 war and the site is now the Fire Station.

The headquarters for the Hertfordshire Yeomanry cavalry was for a time in Hertford and the building is still in use today. It is the headquarters of the county Cadet Force and the local territorial platoon. As the yeomanry was strongest in the north of the county, Hitchin Museum is recognised as being the county's yeomanry museum but there are some items in Hertford Museum to illustrate the town's connection. However, Hertford Museum is home to the Hertfordshire Regiment Collection and collecting related items is an ongoing policy.

In 1908 Lord Haldane reorganised the nation's volunteer forces and the Hertfordshire Regiment was created although its origins are to be found in the Hertfordshire Rifle Volunteers formed in 1859. The new regiment's headquarters was on the corner of Port Hill at the entrance to Hartham Common and has only recently been demolished. The Regiment won national acclaim for bravery in the 1914–1918 war and the soubriquet of the 'Herts Guards', given to it by a national newspaper, has remained. The collection contains assorted uniforms, some of which belonged to leading citizens of Hertford, such as Col. Longmore and Major Barber. Two of its troopers were awarded the Victoria Cross for valour in the 1914–1918 war, one of which is in the Museum. It was awarded to Corporal A.A. Burt, a Hertford gas fitter, and was donated by his daughter in 1979 with the instruction that it was never to leave the town. Burt was in a crowded trench at Cuinchy when a mortar bomb fell in it. He calmly pulled out the pin and threw it out of the trench, undoubtedly saving many lives. Apparently Burt learned that he had been awarded the VC when reading a copy of a national newspaper while waiting at a French railway station. The other Victoria Cross was awarded posthumously to 2nd Lt. F.E. Young of Hitchin. This medal is on display in the Hertfordshire and Bedfordshire Regimental Museum at Luton. However, all the related documents are in Hertford Museum. After the war the two battalions of the Hertfordshire Regiment became part of the newly formed 'Beds and Herts'. However there was such a hue and cry from the eastern part of the county that the Hertfordshire Regiment was reformed with just one battalion. This arrangement continued until 1961 when new legislation merged it with the Bedfordshire Regiment. The core of the Hertfordshire Regiment Collection was placed in the Museum at this time. No doubt this was to make sure

Corporal A.A. Burt, V.C.
(Hertford Museum Collection HETFM:2666.10)

the items stayed in the Regiment's hometown. More changes took place in 1969 which resulted in the Bedfordshire and Hertfordshire Regiment being absorbed into the Royal Anglian Regiment.

Since then the collection has grown with donations and purchases. These include a small attaché case filled by Pte. Cooper with souvenirs of his WWI service in France. Cooper was an observant young man who kept well-penned diaries. He came from Ware and his time in France was an adventure as well a call to serve his country. Another gift is the Gazettes in which Pte. Rodney Stevens is mentioned. These were donated by his sister who was then aged over ninety and living in Wales. Their father had kept a cycle shop in Hertford, which was demolished to create Salisbury Square. She recalled watching, from her bedroom window, Hertford Regiment men marching up Bull Plain en route to the station, where their journey to France would begin. She also recalled her father telling Rodney not to teach his little sister bawdy songs!

Sgt. Alfred J. Branch circa 1940 (Hertford Museum Collection HETFM:1997.24.3.26)

A particularly important item was purchased in 1997. It was the Distinguished Conduct Medal awarded to Act/Sgt. A.J. Branch of Hoddesdon "for conspicuous gallantry when on duty" at Banzuolo Ridge, Italy, in 1944. 'Sonny' Branch, later died in action at the age of twenty-two. A trawl through telephone directories made contact with his brother who was delighted to be able to give the Museum related papers including the telegram notifying their mother of his death, and other ephemera and photographs.

The continuous reorganisation of regiments, as they merge and cover larger and larger recruiting areas, has resulted in historical regimental items being stored a long way from their original home and virtually inaccessible to those who would be most interested in them. Therefore it was decided that they should be deposited in appropriate museums and in October 2000, the Museum received a large donation of assorted and very worthwhile items, from the Bedfordshire and Hertfordshire Regiment and Militia Trust, that had been stored near Colchester.

Readers who may wish to learn more about the County's regimental history are advised to read publications written by Col. John Sainsbury.

Chapter 10

HERTFORD MUSEUM ARCHAEOLOGY
by Clive Partridge

Hertford's recorded roots in archaeology go back some way before even the foundation of the East Herts Archaeological Society in 1898 – this was four years before the founding of the Hertford Museum. Both the EHAS and Hertford Museum owe their beginnings largely to the Andrews. Robert Thornton and William Frampton Andrews were keen amateur archaeologists and local historians. Robert had been an established member of the St. Albans and Hertfordshire Architectural and Archaeological Society for some years before the events of 1898. But both brothers were somewhat dissatisfied with the lack of attention given to work and finds being made in East Herts. They eventually decided to call a meeting in Hertford of all interested persons, with a view to forming a separate society to cover mainly the eastern side of the county. At the meeting were several notable local antiquarians such as J.L. Glasscock and A. Boardman from Bishop's Stortford, on the eastern fringes of the county. They and others were enthusiastic about the proposition and at the meeting it was agreed that such a society should be formed and would be named the East Hertfordshire Archaeological Society.

The first report of the duly constituted society in 1899 records the efforts of the Society's members to recover information about finds in East Herts. At the newly acquired site in Ware for the Allen & Hanbury's factory finds of Roman pottery, coins and other artefacts had been made. These had been recorded by members and the Society made a request to acquire the objects, which was favourably received. These finds were the forerunners of many more important discoveries to be made in the 1940s and then during the major expansion and reconstruction work which began in the mid-70s after the take-over by Glaxo UK.

The establishment of a museum in Hertford had always been one of the aims for the Andrews. During the early years, from 1903, displays of archaeological, ethnographic and local historical material were mounted in their offices in Fore Street. The exhibitions proved to be very popular with local people and the increase in public awareness was reflected in the numbers of new members joining EHAS. In 1909 Robert Andrews assumed the duties of Curator. Three rooms in the offices were given over to the display of exhibits. Meanwhile, William, who was a Borough Councillor, had been campaigning for some years – to little or no avail – for recognition of the importance of a local museum which all the public could visit.

As interest grew more and more local material came to light and was donated to the embryonic museum in Fore Street. In 1913 the brothers made the decision to purchase a property at 18 Bull Plain. They renovated and adapted the premises to provide office space and rooms for the display and storage of material. The new museum was opened to the public in February 1914. During the early years the EHAS meetings were held in the Museum and, of course, the Society's Library was stored there.

After Robert's death in 1926 his son Herbert, who was a librarian at the Victoria & Albert Museum, took on the task of managing the collections. Henry Robins, a retired Hertford businessman and enthusiastic collector of bygones, was appointed Hon. Curator to look after the day to day running of the Museum. Herbert died in 1947 and this proved to be a watershed for the Museum. Now Hertford Borough Council finally agreed to take an active interest in the Museum. At the time, despite the acknowledged importance of the Museum to the people of Hertford and East Hertfordshire, no real effort was made to put the Museum on a proper staffed basis. Instead it was lumped together with other local organisations under the banner and control of the Chief Librarian of the Library Service. In the circumstances it was inevitable that the earlier close links between the Museum and the EHAS should wane somewhat. Little in the way of active fieldwork or excavation was accomplished by the Museum in the following 16 years.

In 1963 the Robinson Report was published, laying down guidelines for the running of Museums and Art Galleries as separate entities from Library Services and similar organisations. To their credit the Borough Council took these recommendations on board and agreed to the appointment of a full time curator. Gordon Davies was appointed in March 1964. Whether by design or chance, the new curator had an archaeological background and the Museum once again began to function as an active participant in the archaeology of East Hertfordshire.

From 1964 onwards the Museum's Excavation Register reveals increasing notes on field walking, watching briefs and recording small scale rescue operations, undertaken in the town and surrounding areas. In the 1970s the Museum had an important part to play in the increasing pace of Rescue Archaeology. The construction of new roads and by-passes and the start of widespread re-development of the town centre put a great strain on the archaeological resources of the Museum and the East Herts Archaeological Society Excavation Group. Money, manpower (not to mention a goodly helping of womanpower) and storage facilities were at a premium.

The EHAS Excavation Group had long been active on an amateur basis, relying on volunteer labour from the Museum and Society members. With the greater need for more rapid reaction to the pace of Rescue Archaeology, the Excavation Group was put on a semi-professional basis by the appointment of a full-time Director with some paid supervisory staff. Nevertheless, the group still relied to a great extent on the members' volunteer efforts and the co-operation of the Museum. The Curator kindly provided storage and work space which was essential for the management of the large volume of finds coming from a number of major excavations.

In 1973–4 several notable events took place. First, the Museum finally appointed as Assistant Curator its own full-time archaeologist, Martin Petchey. He was soon plunged into the deep end of Rescue Archaeology. With staff from the excavation group he carried out a number of excavations in the town and surrounding area.

Secondly, after discussion with the government's Department of the Environment Excavations Section, it was agreed that money would be made available to fund a fully professional unit to be called the Hart Archaeological Unit. At this point Robert Kiln (later to become President of EHAS on the death of Sir John Hanbury) purchased the properties of 15 & 15A Bull Plain – immediately opposite the Museum – and allowed the new unit to establish its headquarters there. This provided much needed room for working areas, offices and some storage space.

Thirdly, at about the same time the Museum acquired the lease of McMullen's old Seed Warehouse in The Wash. This was to prove of enormous benefit to both the Museum and the HAU. The enormous, three storey barn-like building provided ample work space and storage for the Museum and, by the good offices of Gordon Davies, much needed storage and processing areas for the Unit.

Fourthly, in 1974 the HAU embarked on the longest continual running series of Rescue excavations ever carried out in the county. It started when Gordon Davies, who always diligently monitored likely planning applications, noted an application from Redlands Gravel to extract sand and ballast from large areas at Foxholes Farm on the south-east outskirts of Hertford. Initial field walking discovered a whole palimpsest of archaeological features which were revealed when Redlands began the initial procedure of top-stripping the fields – the area now covered by the Foxholes Industrial Estate.

With the help of a grant from Hertford Museum, an initial area excavation revealed a mass of archaeological features, many cutting through or across earlier features. At this point the operation took on a much more urgent dimension. There were many acres of even the initial cleared area to be investigated. Fortunately the recently inaugurated Government Initiative (or Job Creation Scheme) to find temporary work for the long term unemployed, came to our aid. Much of the initial workforce was totally unskilled in archaeological procedures but a willingness to learn and contribute to the team effort was all that was needed. Over the next few years this blend of experienced archaeological supervisors and willing hands, backed up with significant contributions from pupils of Haileybury College and Simon Balle School, accomplished the mammoth task of excavating some 30 hectares of upland gravel areas in advance of extraction. Foxholes eventually proved to be the most productive large scale site excavated to date in Hertfordshire. Many hundreds of features were recorded ranging from the Neolithic, through the Bronze Age, Iron Age, Roman and Saxon periods. The work took nearly eleven years to complete. The results have been published by the author as a monograph entitled *Foxholes Farm – A Multi-Period Gravel Site,* 1989 (Monograph 1 Hertfordshire Archaeological Trust). Since then the importance of the finds has made it prime required reading for students of Field Archaeology.

One of the most spectacular finds was a Roman corn-drying oven. Almost complete, this 4th Century structure was thought worthy of saving from the maw of the gravel draglines. Discussions took place between Redlands Gravel, HAU and Hertford Museum as to the feasibility of total recovery. With much valuable help from the DoE Ancient Monuments Laboratory, John Pryke of Pynfords Building Movers and the kind donation by Redlands Gravel of ready mixed concrete for the base, and provision of flat-bed lorries for transport, we finally lifted the oven (all 16 tonnes of it) in two sections and transported it to the Hertford Museum's newly acquired Seed Warehouse in November 1975. It took approximately a year to rejoin and restore the oven. It is now looked after and conserved by the Museum who open it to the public on selected weekends (in August & September) each year. In 1975 the corndrier was unique in being the first and only Roman corndrier in captivity in the world and still remains so today.

Robert Kiln and Anne Joel inspecting the corndrier in situ at Foxholes Farm, 1975 (Hertford Museum archive)

Over the next 10 years the Museum and Unit cooperated in many areas to their mutual benefit. The Museum lost its Archaeological Assistant Curator in 1975 when Martin Petchey left for pastures new at the recently formed Milton Keynes Archaeological Unit. Owing to cuts in funding the Museum was not able to replace him. Fortunately, not all connections with archaeology were severed. The new

Assistant Curator – Lis Barratt – had previous field excavation experience on sites in Somerset and also as a volunteer with the HAU. When later on in 1975 skeletons were uncovered in Market Square (it is fairly common for the outer margins of early market places to have been used for the interment of bodies) by the contractors of the town centre sewer replacement project, she was able to rescue most of the important parts for examination by the British Museum anthropologists. The skeletons were eventually dated to the late Saxon period c. 900–1066.

These dates are very significant in the known history of this period. We know from the Anglo Saxon Chronicle that Edward the Elder, who had come to the throne in 899 on the death of his father Alfred and had continued his father's campaigns against the Danes, constructed two defended burghs at Hertford at the beginning of his major campaigns against the Danes. The first was on the north side of the River Lea in the area of Old Cross in AD 912 – perhaps a provocative move as the north bank of the Lea was the official boundary of the Danelaw at that time. In 913 he constructed a larger and probably better defended burgh on the south side of the Lea in the general area of The Wash, Bull Plain, Maidenhead Street, Railway Street and the Market Square, Fore Street area. This historic period is one of the most exciting episodes in Hertford's chequered history. Hertford was the kicking off point for one of the most notable campaigns in English history. Edward and his sister Athelflaed began the big push against the Danes which saw them defeat the Danes at Bedford. Thereafter, in one of the finest military operations of its day, brother and sister eventually succeeded in thrusting the Danes back to Northumbria, thus securing most of England from the scourge of the Danes for good.

The Roman corndrier being lifted into the Seed Warehouse, 1975 – photo by kind permission of Stephen Austin Ltd

The Hart Archaeological Unit was forced into retirement in 1986. With the demise of the old Department of the Environment and the advent of English Heritage, the priorities and funding for field archaeology radically changed. Much more emphasis was placed on channelling money into standing monuments – castles, monasteries, abbeys, historic houses, etc. This meant that in Field Archaeology many of the smaller archaeological units were deprived of establishment costs and post-excavation funding which was vital to the ongoing work.

A completely new system of funding came into being. Developers were now obliged to pay for archaeological investigation before final planning permission was granted. Units like the HAU with substantial post-excavation back-logs had little chance of getting funds for the vital ongoing work. The HAU was eventually replaced by the Hertfordshire Archaeological Trust which was initially funded by grants from the County Council and District Councils. HAT took up residence in the McMullen's Seed Warehouse, where it still has its heaquarters under its new name of Archaeological Solutions Ltd. So, albeit in a somewhat diminished way, the co-operation between the Museum and the archaeological unit still exists today.

Lis Barratt excavating Saxon burials in Hertford Market Place, 1975 (Hertford Museum archive)

Over the years this co-operation has enhanced the Museum's collections in more than a local way. This ranges from the unique Roman corndrier to the material on display in the museum from such important sites as Skeleton Green and Foxholes Farm. Though not extensive, the Museum's archaeological exhibits and the reserve collections are, in many cases, second only to those that the British Museum holds. At this notable centenary time the Museum's future looks fairly secure. It is hoped that its historic connections with archaeology will long continue.

Chapter 11

CLOCKS AND SCIENTIFIC INSTRUMENTS
by Edgar Lake

The first person to suggest that Hertford needed a museum was the 5th Marquess Townshend. This was in 1879 and he was addressing a local meeting of the Early Closing Movement. The proposal to close shops at 5 p.m. on Thursdays was a matter of contention. One of the arguments against closing early was that the assistants would not spend their time 'properly'. Lord Townshend took the view that they could spend the extra free time as they wished. He went on to say that with a museum in the town "those with an interest in scientific pursuits would have an opportunity of studying them".

The Victorians had a passion for science. The wealth of the nation had been created by understanding and harnessing the natural world. For the first fifty years of the Bull Plain Museum, the first floor was given over to the display of natural history. It was a study collection. As well as the stuffed birds, mammals and fish there were cabinets of butterflies, moths, birds' eggs, shells, fossils and minerals. In 1899, before the Museum was established, Mr. Wickham of Ware promised a large collection of local fossils and minerals. The Museum owns a fine library of books on natural history dating from a hundred years ago. Time and the clothes moth have destroyed many of the specimens, but a great deal of this collection survives in the Museum store.

Scientific instruments are included in the collection. Perhaps the finest examples are the celestial globe and orrery. These were made by Jeremiah Cleeve of Welwyn in about 1810. An orrery is a clockwork model of the planetary system and the celestial globe is a map of the stars. At one time the two cases were linked. The actual globe was made by J. Newton and is dated 1801. For many years the orrery was demonstrated for interested visitors. It does not currently work, but hopefully one day it will be repaired.

The Museum owns three interesting microscopes. There is a brass Culpepper microscope dated about 1820 by Mackenzie of Cheapside, London, a Nuremberg tripod example and a compound monocular microscope from 1840 by a Manchester optician called Dancer.

An early pioneer with regard to the use of electricity was a local clockmaker, Charles Antonio Maffia. He was born about 1870 and died in 1943. His father came from Italy and he established a shop in Fore Street next door to the Mercury offices.

Orrery of the planetary system and celestial globe, made by Jeremiah Cleeve of Welwyn, about 1800 (Hertford Museum Collection HETFM:1150.1-3). Photograph kindly reproduced by permission of Archaeological Solutions Ltd (previously Hertfordshire Archaeological Trust)

Charles is thought to have been educated at Hertford Grammar School. We know that he was born above the shop. He was passionate about electricity and was the first person in Hertford to use electric light, obtaining the power for his dynamo from the engine at the *Mercury* office next door. He advised Lord Salisbury on the lighting at Hatfield House, which was one of the first great houses to take up the new invention. He made his own telephone and phonograph and he was the first to use wireless in the town.

One of the Museum's great treasures is an electric clock made by Maffia in the early 1900s. He was helped in this project by his friend Charles Baldock of Hastings. It is thought that only four of these clocks were made. It is a traditional clock but is wound by an electric motor powered by a 12-volt battery. Maffia and Baldock had to make their own electric motor to power the clock. This comes into operation once an hour and winds the clock in five seconds. When he died he had two of these clocks in his possession. One was bequeathed to Mrs. Addis; the other to Hertford Museum. Charles Antonio never married. He was devoted to his sister Mary and they rest together in Hertford Cemetery. He was a keen musician and played the violin. Local folk loved to call into his shop just to talk. He was a man with many friends and these included the Faudel Phillips family of Balls Park.

The Museum owns some interesting early electrical equipment. It has a Plate Electrical Machine, a Cylinder Electrical Machine from the 1840s and a Read's Electrical Machine.

The town has produced a number of clockmakers but this is an area in which the collection is weak. Perhaps there is scope for local donations! Three watchmakers were buried in All Saints' Churchyard in the mid 18th Century and it would be good to find examples of their work. John Chamberlain was buried in 1766, Lewis Ferron in 1774 and John Blaney in 1775. John Lawler had a shop at 19 St. Andrew Street from the 1850s to the 1890s. He undertook walking tours, going as far as Scotland and the West Country to repair and overhaul clocks.

One of Hertford's finest buildings was demolished in 1938 to make way for Burton's and a Billiard Hall. This was 'The Old Coffee House Inn'. I suspect that the developers realised that such vandalism was indefensible and allowed Herbert Andrews to remove everything he wanted for the Museum. This included a large faced tavern clock.

Nuremberg Tripod Microscope (Hertford Museum Collection HETFM: 1162)

The collection includes work by Robert Rear, Humphrey Clarke, Samuel Harry, John Marie and Edward Simson. There are no examples of the work of James Field, 1785 to 1865. He was an outstanding clockmaker and founder of the firm that many of us remember as 'Evan Marks'. A fine specimen of his work is to be seen in the Hertford Club.

Perhaps the greatest of all the clockmakers was John Briant, 1749 to 1829. He was born at Exning in Suffolk. From childhood he had a passion for clocks and chimes. It is not known who trained him but he came to Hertford some time before 1780. He cast bells, made turret clocks and also long case clocks. His best-known clocks are the one on the Shire Hall, 1824, and the one in All Saints' Church tower, 1810. The All Saints' clock was made for St Mary's Church in Ware, passed on to the Workhouse in Ware Road (later Kingsmead School) finally arriving at All Saints' in 1970. Briant's output of bells was prodigious. He cast in total 422 and they are in 185 churches. The foundry was on the site now occupied by the Job Centre in Parliament Square. Sadly he died a poor man in the Almshouses at St. Albans. When he died he was brought back to Hertford and buried in All Saints' Churchyard. The

Museum possesses three examples of his workmanship. Two are bells. One is from the turret clock of Hallingbury House in Essex, and is dated 1809 (Dodds No 303). The other was given by John Briant to the Hertford National School in 1824 (Dodds No 438). There is also a longcase clock (Dodds page 188). This is usually on show and welcomes visitors with a gentle tick.

The subject of Hertford clockmakers has yet to be researched. There were interesting links between them. When John Briant retired in 1825, his assistant James Skerman continued the clock making business. This business was eventually taken over by Samuel Harry and continued by his son Harry Harry. Before setting up on his own, Samuel Harry had worked for Edward Simson. Alas it is no longer possible to go out and buy a clock that has been made in Hertford. Finally, it is interesting to note that Charles Maffia foresaw the future. When we do buy a clock these days it usually runs on a battery.

Further Reading:

Science Preserved: A directory of scientific instruments in collections in the United Kingdom and Eire, by Mary Holbrook (1992). Instruments in the Hertford Museum are listed on page 136.

Marquess Townshend's speech to the Early Closing Movement was reported in the *Hertfordshire Mercury* on 3rd May 1879.

John Briant, by H.C.Andrews (1930)

Retirement of Mr. C.A.Maffia, *Hertfordshire Mercury* 5th September 1925

Notes on the Maffia Clock, by Robert Addis 1983, in the Museum collection.

'A Famous Clockmaker, Ralph Lawler', *Hertfordshire Mercury* 25th December 1936.

Hertfordshire Bellfounders, Joyce Dodds (2003).

Chapter 12

THE GEOLOGY COLLECTION
by Margaret Harris

If you had wandered down Ware Road some 10,000 to 1,0000,000 years ago you may have encountered, instead of your neighbour, a woolly mammoth or a hippopotamus. How do we know this? Simply by the remains that have been found in this area and presented to Hertford Museum. One of the most interesting parts of the Museum geology collection is the local material from the Pleistocene period, dating from two million years ago. During this period Britain experienced many changes in climate, when there were times of cold glacial stages with warmer intervals. During the glacial stages, the woolly mammoth, woolly rhinoceros, giant elk and other animals managed to survive. Between the glacial stages, warmer periods occurred, when herds of animals such as hippopotamus, bison and deer thrived. These glacial stages caused extensive gravel and sand deposits and it was in excavating these minerals in the last century that the remains of some of these mammals have been discovered.

Many mammoth remains were found in this area of Hertfordshire, as were hippo, deer and other mammals. The most important site was Grubb's Gravel Pit in the Water Hall Farm area near Essendon, where a quantity of animal bones and teeth were discovered including mammoth, bison, horse, woolly rhinoceros and the famous Hertfordshire Hippo. It is said that Water Hall Farm was the site of the largest hippo finds of the Pleistocene age in Britain. Whilst much of this hippo collection now resides in the Natural History Museum, Hertford Museum has several good specimens, as well as the main collection of mammoth and other animal remains. One particular mammoth tusk found measured more than six feet in length. Much of this collection from Water Hall Farm was presented to the Museum in 1936. Earlier in the 20th century, mammoth remains were found in Ware Road and Mead Lane in Hertford. Several other specimens were discovered in gravel pits locally, and presented over the course of time to the Museum, sometimes by the quarry staff or by local enthusiasts. Fossils and mammoth remains were also found during work on the local railways at the beginning of the last century. Railway engineers gave to the Museum mammoth teeth, sea urchins and other fossils found during the excavations of the Molewood and Bayford tunnels, and the building of the Camps Hill footbridge.

Before this time during the Cretaceous period, some 100 million years ago, Britain was further south, and covered by a warm sea. During the course of the next 30 million years, small organisms died, sank to the bottom of the sea and were gradually compacted to form the chalk which we see all around us in this area. The sea retreated leaving the chalk exposed; this chalk in places is up to 800–1,000 feet thick. The Museum has many fossils that have been found in the chalk, including ammonites, sea urchins and sponges. These sponges are often found as flints formed by the chemical conditions prevailing at the time. Some fossil sponges that the Museum owns are completely spherical and are often taken to be cannon balls, others are sometimes called dog-bone sponges because of their shape.

The rest of the collection is no less fascinating even though much of it was not collected locally. It reflects the interest in Victorian times in scientific matters, especially geology. The founders of the Museum each had a wide range of interests, and in combining these they were able to lay down the foundations of the Museum as we know it today. It is evident from the records that it was Robert Thornton Andrews, one of the founders and the first curator, who had the main geological interest, and he collected from all round Britain as well as locally. Notebooks survive with details of his field trips in local areas, and he not only collected material from various quarries and lime pits, but he also noted down his observations. For example, he would count pebbles and rocks in a section of boulder clay and note their type.

It seems that he was conducting a survey of the erratics found in the boulder clay. An erratic is material carried sometimes for many miles by ice movement and rivers, and he sent many of these specimens to Sir George Fordham who was researching the distribution of erratics in Hertfordshire. As well as going out and collecting himself, he also bought many of the specimens that are in the Museum. The first reference to the purchase by R.T. Andrews of geological items in the Hertford Museum day-books, was in 1901. This referred to the sale by the Royston Institute of a large number of fossils, including sharks' teeth, vertebrae, coprolites and minerals. These were originally from a collection of a Mr. J. Smith of Bassingbourne, presented to the Royston Institute in 1872.

R.T. Andrews also purchased many specimens from fossil and mineral dealers, and would seem to have been very exacting in his standards, as one group of letters testifies. He apparently ordered a quantity of Paris Basin fossils from a Manchester dealer which did not meet his high expectations. The dealer, Mr. Richard Bates, wrote a most hurt letter in which he stated how "painfully shocked" he was in receiving such an unkind letter from Mr. Andrews on the quality of his fossils. However, Mr. Andrews seems to have accepted them as they are listed as being on display soon after.

There are also records in the old day-books detailing many gifts from R.T. Andrews of minerals and fossils to the Museum from all parts of Britain. A large quantity of these specimens was from Derbyshire, such as fluorspar and Blue John. He also seemed to be building up a collection of fossils of the Red Crag formation from the Pleistocene period, including items from Felixstowe, Walton-on-the-Naze and other

78 Hertford Museum Centenary

Photographs of a mammoth tusk from Water Hall Farm gravel pit in 1936   (Hertford Museum Collection: HETFM:6037.268 and, below,HETFM 6037.267)

east coast locations. Many of these collections were probably purchased by him, as the quantities involved are large, but I think he probably also collected personally from various locations, perhaps when on holiday. His interest in things geological also extended to the written word, as he bought many volumes of books on the subject for the Museum library. He also purchased a very fine set of pear wood models of the mineral crystal systems, and a small table-top, inlaid with many polished stones and marbles. It was evident that he was keen to build up a comprehensive geological collection for the Museum. By contrast, William Frampton Andrews, brother and co-founder of the Museum, presented only a few fossils, as his interests were elsewhere, but again, it would seem that he collected them personally. Other members of the family also gave items, probably again collected when on holiday, as many of their gifts came from sea-side resorts such as Ilfracombe, Whitby, Swanage and Scarborough. Amongst these are many ammonites, gryphaea, belemnites and sea urchins. Walter Andrews, who was Bishop of Hokkaido, Japan and brother of R.T. and W. F. Andrews, is recorded as giving a piece of petrified wood in 1903, but it is not known whether the wood was from Japan or not.

In all, Hertford Museum has more than 4,000 specimens in the geological collection, 3,000 being fossils, the rest rocks and minerals. Apart from the items on display at Bull Plain, they are housed in over one hundred wooden drawers in the Museum stores in the Seed Warehouse. A large part of this collection dates from before the 1920s, although the Museum has been adding to it up until the present day. Nearly all these specimens have been catalogued, but the very early Museum records, in common with those from other Museums with old collections, are not complete. For example, several old entries in the day-books might read "a quantity of minerals and fossils" so work is still needed in trying to match up the specimens with the donor, but this may not be possible in some cases.

Apart from the material purchased and collected by the early curators, we have many specimens given by private individuals. Many of these donations date from the late 19th century, some being individual specimens, some collections. For example, we have a very fine group of over forty rocks and minerals from the West Country area, known as the Tom Collection. This includes examples of galena, tourmaline, aragonite and amethyst, among others. There is also reference in the day-books of a large quantity of minerals and fossils from Caer Caradoc in Shropshire, Wales and from the Coal Measures, presented by Mr. J. W. Salter in 1905. Mr. Salter was at one time a palaeontologist to the Geological Survey of Great Britain. An interesting donor from 1915 was Mr L. Partridge, from Little Berkhampstead House, who was a member of the affluent Partridge family, he and his brothers all being successful art dealers. He gave a large collection of polished stones for brooches, as well as many minerals and native metals. The polished stones seem to refer to a collection of about eighty cut and polished agates which the Museum has in store.

As well as large collections, many people gave just one or two specimens, perhaps when giving other miscellaneous items. These donations came from all over the world as well as many from Britain. One interesting gift was of two gold nuggets from the Klondike, presented in 1904 by Mr. Damment. Other curiosities include a meteorite, ploughed up at Perry Wood in 1894 by a Mr. Burgess, and a thunderbolt found by Mr. Peel in Tewin in 1915. A thunderbolt would seem to be in this case a nodule of iron pyrites, although it usually refers to a fossil of a sea animal related to the squid, known as a belemnite. A thunderbolt at one time was thought to be an actual physical object. There are also references to gifts of opals, sapphires, peridots and gold from Australia, dust from Vesuvius, asbestos minerals from Switzerland and rocks from Gibraltar.

Other noteworthy items are two crocodile skulls from the Isle of Wight, ichthyosaur vertebrae, fish remains from Italy and sharks' teeth. The Museum also owns a very good collection of plant material from the Carboniferous period including club mosses and ferns. For example, there is an excellent example of Lepidodendron, with a branch and outgrowths, thought to be fairly uncommon in this condition. There is also reference to a piece of fossil wood from Portland, donated by Mr. Webb from Horns Mill in 1903, and it is said to have been "in the hand of Edward VII".

The best known rock in the Museum collections is Hertfordshire Puddingstone, of which we have many specimens, some cut and polished, some in their natural state. This extremely hard stone consists of well-rounded pebbles in a matrix, resembling currants in a pudding. This rock, known as a conglomerate, is found in the Reading Beds and is formed from sands and gravels deposited over fifty million years ago. There are many legends and superstitions surrounding Hertfordshire Puddingstone, and it was thought to grow, indeed, its other names from long ago included breeding stone and mother stone. Farmers were not usually happy to find Puddingstone in their fields as their equipment was liable to be damaged, so many of these rocks are often seen along the sides of country lanes where they have been placed after removal from farmland. It used to be thought that Puddingstone could help ward off evil spirits by placing it in doorways, but its extreme hardness made it useful in more practical ways. It was used to form tools from as early as the Stone Age, and the Romans fashioned it into small millstones, known as querns – the Museum has several of these in its archaeological collections. Many of the specimens of Puddingstone in the Museum were found as glacial erratics in the gravels, where they had been eroded and transported by the action of ice and water. The polished pieces are extremely attractive as the polish shows the variety of the colours in the pebbles.

The Museum also has many examples of building stones, and whilst these were not collected initially for geological reasons, nevertheless they form an interesting part of the collections. Many of these stones came from the Church of St. Mary the Less, which originally stood on Old Cross in Hertford, and an archway can still be seen near the original site, used at one time as a drinking fountain. The remains were discovered when the foundations of the Hertford Library were excavated in the 1880s, and some were given to the Museum and are now stored in the basement. This church was built of Merstham Stone, a shelly Cretaceous sandstone from Reigate in Surrey, which was often used in medieval times in this locality as Hertfordshire lacks suitable natural building material. The stone was transported to this area by river from Surrey. There is also a medieval coffin in the stores, made of a shelly limestone, possibly Barnack Stone from the Jurassic period. There are various other items including the head of Ceres, once gracing the roof of the Corn Exchange and removed for safety during World War II. This statue, carved in limestone, has weathered very badly.

The Present and Future

Hertford Museum always welcomes visitors to the stores, by appointment, to see the collections not on permanent display, but it is hoped that in the future, funds permitting, storage will be improved to allow easier access, particularly for students and researchers. The Museum also offers an identification service of all those rocks and fossils found in the back garden or souvenirs from the sea-side.

Although the Museum would not now collect geological specimens from such a wide area as the early curators did, good local finds are always welcome. We have also built up over recent years an educational collection of geological material from a wider area to give hands-on opportunities to members of the public, children and adults alike. The most recent additions to this include a collection of polished stones from around the world, and an ichthyosaur footprint from the Swanage area. This handling collection has proved to be very popular, and the Museum hopes to continue adding to it.

Chapter 13

THE R.T. ANDREWS
TRADE TOKEN COLLECTION
by Edgar Lake

During the 17th Century the absence of small change, halfpennies and farthings, made shopping difficult. In 1613 James I attempted to address the problem, and make some money for himself, by selling a patent for producing farthings to Lord Harrington. These could be forged and were not popular. The problem was solved by spontaneous action. From 1648 towns and villages all over the country were supplied with change by the production of local tokens. In some cases a town or city council would issue them, but for the most part they were provided by prominent local traders, innkeepers, grocers and the like. They were men and sometimes women of substance and standing in the local community. Primarily for local use they did in fact move about the country. Vast numbers of tokens were issued over the next 25 years. It was not until 1672 that halfpennies and farthings were issued by the Royal Mint. Even then token use did not end at once, but they were finally banished by a proclamation issued in February 1674.

The diarist John Evelyn predicted that they would be collected by future generations. In due course this happened as they make an important contribution to our knowledge of the local history of the period. Robert Thornton Andrews made a large collection of Hertfordshire trade tokens and he presented it to the Museum. It consists of 366 tokens, most of which are in very fine condition.

The Victorian period was the heyday for token collection. William Boyne FSA published a three-volume work on the subject in 1858. This is in the Museum library. In 1889 George Williamson published a revised edition of Boyne. In every county he sought the assistance of the local expert, which for Hertfordshire was R.T. Andrews who is described as 'Sub-Editor and Collaborateur'. Many of his entries are detailed, providing a wealth of historical background on the issuers. Edward Aynsworth of Bishop's Stortford and Felix Calvert of Furneaux Pelham have a page each. The bulk of the entries are marked with an asterisk and this indicates that the token is in the Andrews' collection.

The Museum copy of Williamson is from a signed limited edition. It was issued in two volumes but R.T.Andrews had it rebound into four. It was interleaved and contains his later notes. Williamson listed 226 tokens for Hertfordshire. Subsequent to publication of the book R.T.Andrews identified a further 12. They still turn up from time to time. In 1964 an unknown Watton-at-Stone token was found in a ploughed field. It was issued by Katherine Alleyn in 1668. She was a woollen draper and in 1664 had appeared in court for trading without having served as an apprentice. The incident it seems did not affect business. Fifty places are listed as issuing tokens but from later finds four more have been identified; Batchworth Bridge, Elstree, Stanstead Abbots and Watton-at-Stone. None of the town councils in Hertfordshire issued pieces.

Tokens were mainly made of brass or copper. For the most part they were round but could be square, octagonal, diamond or heart shaped. Examples of octagonal ones are those of John Cowlee of St. Albans (1/2d) and Ann Brittaine of Bishop's Stortford (1/2d). Sam Goodaker of Cheshunt 1668 (1/2d) and James Hannell of Redbourn 1669 (1/2d) both had heart shaped tokens.

A farthing and a halfpenny token were issued by Edward Aynsworth at the Reindeer in Bishop's Stortford. Inscriptions often included the wife's initial and the farthing has E.E.A. on the reverse. Elizabeth, known as Betty, lived in Cambridge when Samuel Pepys was a student there. She was banished from the city for being a procuress. Pepys and his wife twice stayed at the Reindeer. Elizabeth Pepys was quite unaware that her husband knew the landlady. Pepys wrote of Betty: "lived heretofore at Cambridge and whom I know better than they think for. She was the woman that among other things was great with my cozen, Barnston of Cottenham, and did use to sing to him and did teach me 'Full Forty Times Over', a very lewd song, a woman they are well acquainted with and is here what she was in Cambridge, and all the good fellows of the country came hither." Later in the diary Pepys records that Betty had thoughts of going to London. He did not approve. "I believe she will be mistaken for it, for it will be found better for her to be chief where she is than to have little to do at London." She stayed in Bishop's Stortford and was buried in the churchyard in 1686. It was no doubt a busy inn, hence the two tokens.

There are 19 tokens known for Bishop's Stortford. The spelling of the place name varies and is redolent of the dialect of the day. It appears as Bishop Starford, Bishop Startford, Bishopstaford and in one instance as a rebus with Stortford below a bishop's

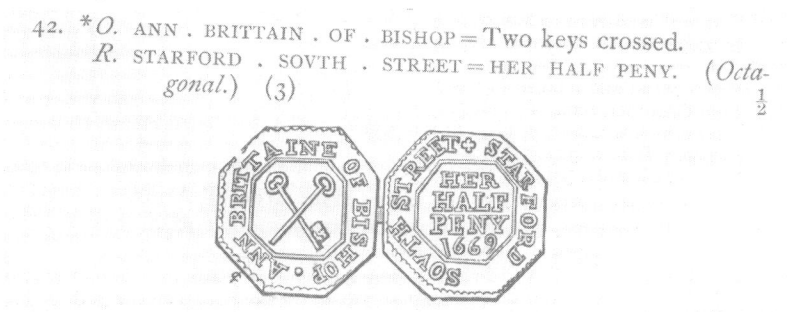

42. *O. ANN . BRITTAIN . OF . BISHOP = Two keys crossed.
    R. STARFORD . SOVTH . STREET = HER HALF PENY. (Octagonal.) (3) $\frac{1}{2}$

Bishop's Stortford Trade Token: 'Ann Brittain of Bishop Starford South Street, Her Half Peny.' (from Boyne's Trade Tokens, Vol.1 Pt. 1, George C. Williamson, 1889)

bust (William Chandler 1/4d). Peterborough had five tokens and the name is spelt in ten different ways. The first octagonal example in the County came from Bishop's Stortford. These were halfpennies issued by Ann Brittaine of the Crossed Keys. Simon Rutland was a grocer and in 1671 his name appears as one of the overseers of the poor. He issued a farthing token showing the grocers' arms, i.e. three groups of three cloves divided by a chevron. Tokens link with three other interesting areas of study; heraldry, inn signs and shop signs.

Only nine tokens are known for Hertford. Three issuers served as Mayors of the Borough. Joseph held office in 1660, was a grocer and issued a farthing. When in 1664 Thomas Noble died and left money for the poor of the town, one of the trustees of his will was Joseph Browne. George Seely, another grocer, was Mayor in 1664. On his token of 1652 the name of the town is spelt as it should be pronounced; 'Harford'.

105. *O*. THOMAS . LOWE = The Drapers' Arms.
R. IN . HARFORDE . 1668 = HIS HALFE PENNY. (5)

Trade Token: 'Thomas Lowe, The Drapers Arms, in Harforde, 1668, his Halfe Penny'

Thomas Prat was Mayor in 1669. He was landlord of the Chequer Inn, on the Post Office site in Fore Street. It was owned by the Borough Council who had bought it in 1629 as a means of investing some money being held on behalf of the poor. It was an important property and the site of the town cockpit. In 1656 a puritan council decided to remove the cockpit. Thomas Prat had invested £10 in it and it was agreed that he should be reimbursed, but the money was never paid and when in 1665 he complained the cockpit was returned to him. His farthing token depicts the chequer board. Thomas included the initials of his wife Mary and the reverse reads 'IN HERTFORD T.M.P.'. With every vestige of the Chequer gone, the token remains the only tangible relic of a once popular hostelry.

The grocer William Carter had served as apprentice to Joseph Browne. He did not include his wife's initials on his farthing token. His name appears frequently in local records as an 'appraiser', that is someone who would value personal property in connection with a will. Grocers as the main traders of the day were well placed to carry out this duty. In 1663 he was referred to in the will of Widow Whison "and my will and meaneing is that my loveing friend William Carter shall pay noe use nor Interest for any money which he hath of mine in his hands". He served on the Borough Council but was removed in 1662 for refusing to take the oath of allegiance. At least

103. O. WILLIAM . CARTER = The Grocers' Arms.
R. GROCER . IN . HARTFORD = W . C.   (5)

Trade Token: 'William Carter, The Grocers' Arms, Grocer in Hartford, W.C.'

two Quakers issued tokens. John King, grocer, issued a farthing in 1652. Abraham Rutt was an ironmonger and his farthing was produced in 1666. Both were removed from the Borough Council in 1662. They were prosecuted for not attending their parish churches and both spent 31 weeks in prison. Dr. Rowe speculates that they were persecuted because of their wealth and prominence in the local community. An attempt was made to confiscate their property but this failed. Robert Stothard was Sergeant-at-Mace in 1666. His name is spelt Stadder on his farthing. He was landlord of the Black Swan in West Street. This lovely old pub was destroyed to make way for the new road.

Twelve tokens are known for Ware. Surprisingly, there does not appear to have been one for the White Hart which was then the home of the Great Bed. One was issued for the Saracen's Head, the bed's later home. The subject has many unanswered questions. Was Ware a busier town than Hertford? To find the answer we would need to know in what quantities the various tokens were produced. Many of the villages had just one token, examples being Eastwick, Kimpton and Lemsford.

Designs were usually simple and functional. The name of the issuer is given and the place. On the halfpenny the amount is often given, and the date. The sign of the inn or trade is displayed and the reverse has the issuer's initials, often with the wife's initials as well. There are some very attractive pieces. Thomas Turney of Hemel Hempstead issued a halfpenny in 1664. On the reverse he had a lily between his initials. William Litchfield and John Pile of Bushey issued a joint token in 1669. On

100. *O. THOMAS . TVRNEY . 1664 = HIS HALF PENY.
R. IN . HEMELL . HEMPSTEED = T . T and a lily.   (2)

Trade Token: Thomas Turney, 1664 His Half Peny in Hemell Hempsteed, T.T.

O. WILL . LITCHFIELD . OF . BVSHEY = A lion rampant, ing an arrow.
R. IOHN . PILE . OF . BVSHEY = A malt-shovel. 1669. (2

The joint Trade Token issued by Will Litchfield and John Pile of Bushey, 1669

his side of the halfpenny John Pile had a simple design of a malt shovel in the middle of the date.

At Marlborough in Wiltshire, John Hammond had a book on his token. History records that when the Royalists took the town in 1642 they spent three hours feeding a fire with Hammond's books. The tokens were issued in a time of great political upheaval. Every piece has a story and there is still much to discover about the people who provided them. In the introduction to his book Williamson wrote that they are "a remarkable instance of a people supplying their own needs by an illegal issue of coinage, and in this way forcing a legislature to comply with demands and requests at once just and imperative. Tokens are essentially democratic; they were issued by the people, and it is of the people that they speak".

Further reading

George Williamson's book remains the best work on the subject. It is little used by local historians, but the R.T.Andrews' notes in the Hertfordshire section provide much useful information – George C. Williamson, *Boyne's Trade Tokens,* 1889.

The First Hertford Quakers by Dr. V.A.Rowe (1970) contains material on John King and Abraham Rutt.

Lifestyle and Culture in Hertford, Wills and Inventories 1660–1725, edited by Beverly Adams (1997) gives a vivid insight into everyday life of the period.

Trade Tokens by J.R.S Whiting (1971) is a useful reference book.

Some writers refer to tokens having a 30-year span of use. This is because they continued to be issued in Ireland until 1679.

Chapter 14

FRIENDS OF HERTFORD MUSEUM
by Alan White

On Monday 12th October, 1981, a meeting was held in a house in Bengeo. The six people present called themselves a steering committee. Mrs.A. Hunter was elected chairman for the meeting and she was joined by Mrs.E. Stenning, Mrs.V. Cunneen and Mr.C. Partridge. Miss E. Barratt attended to represent the Hertford Museum and Mr.C. Lee represented the East Herts Archaeological Society. The minutes of the meeting state:

> Mrs. Hunter outlined the purpose of the Friends of the Museum, which was to raise funds in a dignified way. To help promote the Museum to the general public at large. Make Hertford people aware that this is 'their' Museum. Voluntary group of interested people prepared to assist the Curator and staff in an unqualified way, e.g. help with the donkey work of mounting exhibitions, cleaning, security, manning, etc. Money raised to be used by the Trustees for use as they see fit for the Museum, or to assist with special purchases and projects.

The minutes go on to mention a fund-raising preview of the 'From Seed to Harvest' exhibition at which cider, apple juice and wholemeal bread and cheese would be served; a Christmas bazaar at which the Hertford Art Society would be asked to mount a small exhibition and a 'Yuletide Gathering' during which the Lea Valley Mummers would sing carols.

"Not much has changed," one might say. Mrs. Hunter's outline proved to be a firm foundation on which to base the constitution of the Friends and even the programme of fund-raising activities is recognisable over twenty years on. By January, the Treasurer was able to report that the Christmas bazaar had made a profit of £84.78, the Yuletide Gathering £46.42 and £14 had been received in membership fees, set at £1 per annum.

On 25th March 1982, the public inaugural meeting was held at the Museum Annexe. Sixteen members attended and Mrs. Hunter passed the chair over to Cyril Heath, the well-known local historian and reporter on the local newspaper the *Hertfordshire Mercury*. However, at the election of officers, Mrs. Hunter regained the chair unopposed. The first mention of 'money raised' being used 'as they see fit for the Museum' appears in the minutes of the meeting of 22 April 1982:

Museum Cats it was decided that the sum of £41 be set aside for the treatment and care of the cats so as to help ensure the control of any further increase or incursion by other cats on the Museum garden.

In November of that year, however, a more substantial and significant contribution was made, '£250 to the purchase of an early British gold coin'.

Amongst the expected and inevitable activities listed in those early minutes – exhibition previews, jumble sales, garden parties, cream teas, craft markets – one occasionally finds mention of a fresh idea, a seed sown that was to grow and become a familiar tree in the Friends' landscape. In January 1983: "The subject of the Friends visiting other groups, as ourselves, to exchange ideas and encourage contact and co-operation was discussed …"; in September 1983: "There was a suggestion that the Friends might organise a Collectors' Corner, where members and interested parties might like to show their own collections of postcards, coins and memorabilia"; in March 1985: "Mr. Davies (curator) has kindly agreed to lead one of his guided walks around Hertford" and "the idea of holding a special day, when people could bring their 'finds' to the Museum for identification, was broached. But various complications were foreseen."

There are other things that never seem to change. "The Chairman wishes it to be known that she would like to resign the office and if anyone would like to be considered and would be willing to take over, please put forward the nomination," said Ann Hunter in 1983. She was still being re-elected in 1986, although it was at the AGM in that year that Norman Coyston was elected Vice-Chairman. He duly became Chairman and continued in the post until Baden Brown succeeded him in 1993. Alan White took over in 1997.

It was during the mid eighties that the Friends fell into the habit of having monthly talks from a variety of speakers with interests and expertise in aspects of local history or museum-related topics – Lieut.-Col. Sainsbury on the Home Guard, James Barber on his family firm, founded in 1875. By the end of the century, this had almost come to be regarded as the Friends' *raison d'être* and it took Colin Dawes, the consultant engaged to investigate the Museum's future, to remind us of our obligations under our constitution and put us back on the right track.

Almost the only 'donkey work' that had been undertaken in the Friends' history was the cataloguing of the Museum's postcard collection, a long and valuable contribution but one completed by only a handful of volunteers. The Friends had, however, represented the Museum on various occasions – the now defunct Amwell Steam Rally, the Carnival parade, Medieval Night and the Hertford Fun Day. More recently, increasingly popular Saturday afternoon teas in the Museum garden and open days at the Seed Warehouse have been staffed by the Friends.

Colin Dawes's report stimulated a great deal of volunteer activity, almost, it has to be said, independently of the Friends organisation, although many of those involved were members. Positive cross-fertilisation between the volunteers and the Friends has enabled us to shift the emphasis back towards hands-on assistance, but more needs to be done.

The Friends may be proud, though, of the contributions they have made to the Museum's equipment and collections over the years. Talks and presentations have been enhanced by the slide and overhead projectors provided by the Friends. And an impressive list of artefacts has found its way into the displays as a result of financial contributions:

The purchase of a Rowlandson watercolour painting of a Hertford scene was bought with the assistance of a donation of £200 and £50 went towards the cost of a glass case for the Napoleonic flag, which had been restored.

In March 1990, the Treasurer reported that: "A £378 surplus for the year became a £21.53 deficit because of the donation to the Museum towards the purchase of the silver 'penny'." In November: "We are contributing £420 this year towards the cost of [restoration of] the Railway Street panels."

At the annual general meeting of 1992, it was reported that £200 had been donated for 'sword and palstave'. A rare Roman guild ring was offered to the Museum in 1995 and the Friends readily agreed financial assistance of £350.

In 1998, the Chairman was able to report that, with the Friends' help, the Museum's acquisition of a Distinguished Conduct Medal awarded to Acting Sergeant Alfred J. Branch during the Second World War had been deeply appreciated by Sergeant Branch's family, who supplemented the item with photographs, documents and contemporary newspaper reports.

As recently as February, 2003, the Museum's centenary year, the *Hertfordshire Mercury* was able to report that, with funding from the Friends of Hertford Museum, a Roman gold ring of the 2nd or 3rd century AD, discovered by a detectorist in High Cross, would take its place in a forthcoming 'At Home with the Romans' exhibition.

The Friends of Hertford Museum are rightly proud of their achievements but are far from complacent. They need to campaign to increase their membership, wanting particularly to attract younger members, to undertake more fund-raising and to put more effort into using their varied skills more directly in the Museum's work.

Chapter 15

LOOKING FORWARD
by Helen Gurney

Over the past one hundred years, Hertford Museum has developed and changed and most of those developments you can read about in this book. One development which you will not have read about until now is our plans for the future.

In 2003, Hertford Museum celebrates its centenary, and embarks upon a new chapter in its development. Everyone involved with the museum is aware of the success that new physical changes have brought, whether it be a re-designed garden, or a new entrance area or even simply a new temporary exhibition or display. The centenary marks the beginning of a development project to bring the museum into this century.

A professional review was undertaken in 2000, which flagged up many areas for improvement to the existing building or the possibility of moving the museum to another site. However, many will agree that the site of the museum in 18 Bull Plain, is a familiar one that people can find easily, or pop into on their way home from work.

Admittedly, it does have its shortcomings, such as insufficient parking and its size, but the present site of the museum is an integral part of the history and the development of the museum. Therefore, it was decided by the Trustees in 2002, that the museum would stay in its present location for the foreseeable future, and that we would make sure that we improve the building to ensure the museum's success as a service to the community.

The Present Situation

Have you ventured upstairs to the first floor of the museum? The only way to access this is by the central staircase. Once at the top, you are greeted by a wall and two side doors. The door on the right brings you into the popular and ever-changing activity room, whilst the door on the left takes you into the main open display space which has snippets of local history in a jumbled and rather academic manner.

Until the Centenary Exhibition this year, the first floor galleries had not witnessed any dramatic changes over the last seventy five years.

Many visitors think that this lack of change is all part of the Museum's charm. However, staff and trustees are aware that to attract visitors, both old and new we need to make essential changes so that visitors who walk through the door get

*Photograph showing first floor displays prior to the Centenary Exhibition which opened in August 2003.
Below: the first floor galleries in 1918, R.T. Andrews seated
(Hertford Museum Collection HETFM: 6036.145)*

92   Hertford Museum Centenary

something from their visit, such as enjoyment, a spur of interest or even learning. The service we provide to visitors is all part of our mission statement:

> to collect, preserve and interpret evidence of the history of the county town and district of East Hertfordshire for the interest, enjoyment and understanding of the local community and other visitors

The Need

Many people whom I have escorted upstairs to show them something in particular have often commented 'I never knew you had an upstairs' or 'I have seen all this before, it hasn't changed since I was a child'. Many people are unable to climb the stairs that take them to the first floor gallery.

This demonstrates two essential needs:

1. Ensure that when visitors go upstairs, they see something new and inspiring every visit
2. Make it possible for ALL visitors to reach the first floor.

The Big Picture

1. Re-display

Did you know that Hertford Museum cares for over 50,000 objects in its collection? Did you also know that only about 3-5% are presently on display? This is actually quite a reasonable number for most museums, but what is important to note here is the frequency with which we change our displays.

By re-displaying the first floor area, we hope to show visitors more of what Hertford Museum has in its stores and more importantly, portray the varied and exciting history and culture of Hertford. We can do this by using the display space more effectively by:

- New higher capacity display cases which allow viewing from all different perspectives and heights

- Objects on open display to enable visitors to use all their senses, not just sight.

2. Access

Visitors to Hertford Museum can enjoy an attractive shop and entrance area, a temporary exhibition space that changes on average every two to three months, as well as a ground floor display reflecting Hertfordshire life. They can also enjoy a Jacobean-style garden or wander upstairs to look at the displays or use the activity room.

Not everyone is able to wander upstairs. The stairs present a barrier to enjoyment. A large part of this development project is to ensure that all visitors enjoy access to all areas of the museum. We aim to do this by providing a lift to take visitors up and down through the building. As the building dates back to the 17th century and is Grade II listed, we have to be very careful about planning permission. We will be working with East Hertfordshire District Council and English Heritage to make sure that the installation of a lift is acceptable.

Who will pay for this?

For this project to be truly effective, the museum must not resort to giving a 'cat's lick' to the first floor galleries. The staff, trustees, volunteers and Friends will all be involved in this project and will be working with designers, project managers, architects, surveyors and consultants in order to produce a top quality and long lasting solution.

We estimated (in 2002) that the total cost of refurbishment and the installation of a lift would cost in the region of £600,000.

The Heritage Lottery Fund has been approached and is keen to promote projects which will 'make sure that everyone can learn about, have access to and enjoy their heritage'. It is hoped that it will be able to provide financial assistance for part of this project, but we will be relying also on public donations and sponsorship.

Since the museum was opened in 1903, admission has always been free. The museum is grateful to Hertford Town Council and East Herts District Council for their financial support to help cover the running costs of the museum. We are always keen to accept donations to help us provide a better service through events, exhibitions and education.

The Centenary Year

2003 provides a starting point with which to embark upon this exciting project and we very much hope you will see and approve the changes taking place. Hertford Museum needs your support in many ways.

If you would like to help, or you would like to let us know what you think, then please do contact the Curator on **01992 582686**.

INDEX

Addis Ltd. 50, 73
Addis, Robert 75
Addis, Robin 45
All Saints' Church 7, 12, 33, 39, 49, 56, 63, 74
Allen & Hanbury Ltd. 66
AMSSEE 23, 24
Andrews, Bishop Walter 10, 13, 46, 79
Andrews, Dr. Samuel Percy 13
Andrews family 6–13
Andrews, Herbert Caleb 12, 38, 39, 41, 67, 74, 75
Andrews, Robert Thornton 6, 10, 13, 14, 59, 66, 77, 82, 91
Andrews, William Frampton 6, 11, 13, 14, 47, 56, 58, 60, 66
Austin, Stephen 60
Aynsworth, Edward 82

Baker, William Robert 48
Balls Park 11, 73
Barber, James 88
Barratt, Elisabeth 70, 71, 87
Beadle House 31
Bengeo 87
Bennett, Rosemary 3, 6, 23, 56, 63
Benson, Annette 58
Bickerton, W., FRZS 53, 54
Bishop's Stortford 66, 82, 83
Blake, George 53
Blaney, John 74
Boardman, A. 66
Boer War 51
Boyne, William FSA 82
Bramfield 8
Branch, A/Sgt. A.J., D.C.M. 51, 65, 89
Briant, John 74
Bridgeman, Charles 12
Brown, Baden 88
Brown, Edward A. 57
Bull Inn 32, 56
Bull Plain 6, 11, 14, 16, 22, 30, 72, 90
Burt, Corporal A.A., V.C. 51, 64

Bushey 85
Butcherley Green 17

Calvert, Felix 82
Cambridge 83
Carrington, John 9, 32
Cartledge, George 33
Castle Street 7, 24
Chappell, Frank 37
Chauncy, Sir Henry 17, 58
Cheshunt 83
Christ's Hospital School 52
Cleeve, Jeremiah 72, 73
Cooper, Private 65
Cormack, Patrick MP 26, 27
Cowper School 54
Coyston, Ida 26
Coyston, Norman 88
Cromwell, Oliver 7
Cunneen, Mrs. V. 87
Cunningham, Doll 34

Daguerreotypes 48
Davies, Dr. John 32
Davies, Gordon 16, 26, 49, 67, 68, 88
Dawes, Colin 88
Dickens, Charles 56
Dodds, Joyce 75
Drapentier, Jan 58
Drill Hall, Port Hill 51
Drury, Andrew & Andrews, John 58

East Herts Archaeological Society 31, 55, 66, 87
East Herts District Council 26, 50, 93
Eastwick 85
Edward the Elder 70
EHDFAS 26
Elsden family 16, 49, 51, 52, 53
Elstree 83
English Heritage 17, 71, 93
Every, Sheila 26

Ferron, Lewis 74
Festival of Britain 53
Folly, The 11, 12
Folly Island 7, 8, 9, 11, 31
Fordham, Sir George 77
Fore Street 6, 7, 10, 12, 14, 15, 24, 84
Foster, Allen 52
Fox Talbot 48
Foxholes Farm 24, 68, 71
Frampton Street 11
Friends of Hertford Museum 23, 87
Froissart, Jean 56
Furneaux Pelham 82

Gascoyne Way 49
Geall, Don 36
George, Andrea 28
Gerish, W.B. 55
Glasscock, J.L. 66
Graveson, William 53
Gray, Sarah 24, 28
Green, Len 54
Green, Thomas 12
Gregory, James 33
Gurney, Helen 3, 43, 90

Haileybury College 68
Hale, Richard 14
Harris, Colin 3, 5
Harris, Margaret 3, 47, 76
Harry, Samuel 75
Hart Archaeological Unit 68, 71
Heath, Cyril 52, 87
Hemel Hempstead 85
Hertford and District Camera Club 49, 53
Hertford Art Society 87
Hertford Borough Council
    6, 11, 12, 24, 41, 42, 53, 67, 84
Hertford Castle 48
Hertford Civic Society 5, 20, 22, 26
Hertford Club 17
Hertford Dramatic and Operatic Society 61
Hertford Grammar School 73
Hertford School of Art 57
Hertford Town Council 25, 52, 93
Hertfordshire Archaeological Trust 24, 25,
    27, 71, 73

Hertfordshire Archives and Local Studies 61
Hertfordshire County Council 22, 23
Hertfordshire Mercury 14, 29, 33, 52,
    60, 75, 87, 89
Hertfordshire Puddingstone 80
Hertfordshire Regiment 51, 61, 63
Hertfordshire Yeomanry 64
Hertingfordbury 8, 48
Hill, Thomas 20
Hitchin 64
Hoare, Walter 33
Hoddesdon 65
Home Guard 51
Horns Mill 80
Howarth, Alan MP 29
Hunter, Mrs. A. 87

Japan 10, 11, 13, 42, 46, 79
Jevons, Henry 33
Joel, Anne 69
Johns, Capt. W.E. 28, 52
Johnson, 'Dinks' 35, 40, 41
Jones, Nick 25

Kiln, Robert 28, 68, 69
Kimpton 85
Kingham, Dr. Diana 20, 26, 28
Kirby, Ann 3, 22

Lake, Edgar 3, 39, 72, 82
Lawler, John 74
Layston crucifix 4
Le Hardy, William 41
Lee, Colin 87
Lee Navigation 8
Lemsford 85
Literary Institute, The 61
Little Berkhamsted 9
Lombard House 14, 30, 32, 39, 41

Maffia, Charles Antonio 72, 75
Maidenhead Street 56
Maidenhead Yard 24
McMullen's Brewery 50, 68, 71
Mead Lane 76
Methodism 8
Mill Bridge Rooms 24

Nall-Cain, James 3, 14
natural history 72
New River, the 11
New Zealand 46
Newell, Revd. Robert H. 57
Newton, Henry 52
Nicholls, Arthur 58
Norden, John 14, 17, 21

Old Coffee House Inn 74
Old Cross 6, 80
Ollis, Mary 35

Paine, Crispin 23
Pamphilon family 34, 35
Partridge, Clive 3, 66, 87
Pepys, Samuel 83
Perowne, Revd. 63
Perugini, Kate 56
Petchey, Martin 68, 69
Pioneer Hall 12
Plymouth 7
Prout, Samuel 58
Punch 58
Purkis, Jean 3, 30

Quakers 85
Quince, Joe 35

Railway Street 22, 42
Redbourn 83
Robins, Henry 12, 67
Roman corn-drier 69, 70
Rowe, Dr. V.A. 85, 86
Rowlandson, Thomas 27, 29, 56, 57, 89
Ruffles, Peter 27, 35, 37

Sainsbury, Col. John 65, 88
St. Albans 11, 66, 74, 83
St. Mary the Less 6, 80
Salter, J.W. 79
Seed Warehouse 22, 24, 26, 43, 68, 70, 79
Sele Mill 56
Siam (Thailand) 46
Simon Balle School 54, 68
Skeleton Green 71

Skerman, James 75
Sneeby photographer 15, 50, 52
Speed, John 59
Standon Militia 63
Stanstead Abbots 83
Stenning, Mrs. E. 87
Stevens, Pte. Rodney 65
Sueter, Rear Admiral Sir Murray 42
Synod of Hertford (673 AD) 24

Tate, John 56
Taylor, F.W., the Muffin Man 50
The Folly, Hertford 11
Towers, George 32, 56
Townsend, Simon 26
Townshend, Marquess 72

Underwood, Thomas 56

Van Hage's Garden Centre 26
Victoria and Albert Museum 12, 29

Waltham Cross 11
Ware 23, 66, 74, 85
Ware Road 45, 76
Water Hall Farm 78
Water Hall Farm, Essendon 76
Watton-at-Stone 83
Webb's Newsagents 37
Welwyn 72
Wesley, John 7
West Street 9, 56, 58, 85
Westall, William & Richard 56
White, Alan 3, 87
Wilcox, James 58
Williamson, George 82
Wood, Starr 33, 58
Woolwich Docks 9
World War II 11, 12, 40, 44, 51, 81, 89

Young, 2nd Lieut. F.E., V.C. 51, 64

Zeppelin L16 33